From Zero to Business:
How to Start a Business and Raise Millions in Funding

Joseph Hogue

About this Book

Hard work and passion are no longer enough for small business success!

Small business funding collapsed along with the rest of the financial system in 2008 and has never recovered. More than $30 billion in traditional business loans has yet to return to the market.

More than half of business owners report a lack of financing options and nearly a third say they may be pushed out of business for lack of funding.

As always happens in a free market, new solutions have emerged to overcome hurdles in the old way of doing things. A new model of business financing has been born, staged-funding through alternative finance.

This book is about that new model of business funding and how to build your business strategically.

You'll learn first how to create a business plan from the executive summary through marketing and making the financial projections that will impress investors.

We'll then cover the four stages of business funding and real-world examples of business owners that have used the new model to create and drive their small biz dreams.

Each chapter includes detail on one of the four funding sources as well as how to get the best deals. You'll get a comprehensive look at the advantages and limits of each stage and how to use each one successively to grow your business.

You'll be able to set realistic goals for each stage of funding as well as how to leverage your progress in the next stage.

As an investment analyst for a venture capital firm, I've seen exactly what it takes to build a business from the ground up and what you need to get funded. I've helped business owners detail their business plan to uncover the source of their competitive advantage and how to present their case for funding. As an entrepreneur, I've used this same process to raise money and grow my own business.

In this book you'll learn:

- Seven business plan essentials and how to build a complete strategy from start to finish. (pg. 8)

- How to impress investors with your financial statements without being an accountant. (pg. 21)

- The truth about government business grants and how to use loans to jump-start your dream. (pg. 35)

- How to take your business to the crowd for funding and viral marketing. (pg. 51)

- How to find big money investors and how to rock your presentation. (pg. 90)

- The top 10 business myths and mistakes that will crush your chance for success. (pg. 117)

Crowd101.com is your source for small business tips and funding through the crowd revolution. I use my experience on both sides of the table, as an entrepreneur and as a venture capital analyst, to give you the information you need to start and grow your small business dream. Crowd101 isn't just a crowdfunding site but a community for small business owners to learn about different funding sources and how to build a crowd around their business.

Joseph Hogue, CFA

Born and raised in Iowa, Joseph Hogue graduated from Iowa State University after serving in the Marine Corps. He worked in corporate finance and real estate before starting a career in investment analysis. Mr. Hogue has appeared on Bloomberg as an expert in emerging market investing and has led a team of equity analysts at a venture capital firm. His investment analysis has been featured in advisor newsletters, institutional research reports and in the financial press.

He holds the Chartered Financial Analyst (CFA) designation, the gold standard for ethical and professional conduct in investment management.

From Zero to Business: How to Start a Business and Raise Millions in Funding

ISBN-13 # 978-0-9971112-3-1 (paperback)

ISBN-13 # 978-0-9971112-2-4 (digital)

Contents

You Have a Dream, Now you Need Money

Small businesses of less than 500 employees make up the life-blood of our economy, accounting for 65% of the net new jobs created. Just over half a million new businesses are started each month. More than half are home-based and 80% employ a single hard-charging entrepreneur.

Running your own business is truly the American dream and your chance at financial freedom. As a business owner, you'll work harder than you ever have before but you'll be in control of your own success. The satisfaction you get from your entrepreneurial effort is what drives you and will help you to push on.

But hard work and passion isn't always enough. Just half of new businesses survive through five years and only 25% are left after a decade.

More than half of the respondents to a recent Manta survey said they didn't have enough sources of business funding and a third said they might be forced out of business for lack of funds.

Six years after the collapse of the global financial system, small business loans in the United States were not even close to recovering prior highs. Loans of less than $1 million amounted to $302 billion through 2014 were still 10% lower than the 2008 high. Worse is the fact that start-up loans of under $100,000 are off even more, lower by 20% compared to before the Great Recession.

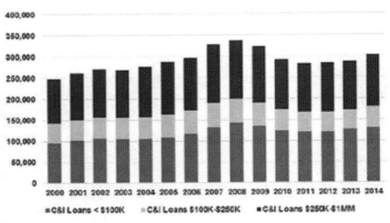

Loans to Small Businesses by FDIC-Insured Institutions in 2000 – 2014, by Loan Size (in $ million)

Source: FDIC.

The FDIC reports that banks are approving less than half (49.6%) of loan applications from small business owners. Some of the drop in traditional bank funding can be attributed back to new regulations and controls on the financial system. Requirements from Dodd-Frank and Basel III regulations mean that banks must hold on to more cash rather than loan it out and compliance costs to make loans has jumped. It now costs a community bank just as much to originate a loan of $250,000 or less as it does to write a loan of more than a million dollars. These higher costs and requirements have taken the profit motive out of small business lending, shutting smaller banks and leaving business owners with fewer funding options.

But the financial crisis isn't completely to blame for the drought in small business loans. The number of community banks in the United States has been tumbling for more than 30 years. The largest mega-banks have been buying up smaller rivals. These larger banks have been less interested in making smaller, community-focused loans and more interested in wealth management and investing products.

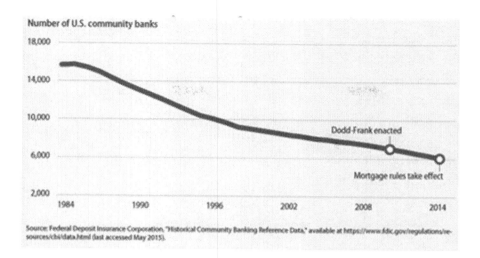

Number of U.S. community banks

Source: Federal Deposit Insurance Corporation, "Historical Community Banking Reference Data," available at https://www.fdic.gov/regulations/re-sources/cbi/data.html (last accessed May 2015).

It doesn't look like the environment for business loans will improve anytime soon. The Federal Reserve started raising its benchmark interest rate in December 2015, threatening to push loan rates higher over the next several years. Only about 80% of the rules around the Dodd-Frank law have been formalized and it's likely that future legislation will further restrain loan growth.

As is always the case in a free market, new solutions are created when hurdles appear in the traditional model. Alternative sources of business funding through peer lending and crowdfunding have surged over the last several years. Those still clinging to the old paradigm have tagged the new system of finance as 'alternative' but funding through these sources is doubling each year and soon to be the mainstream model for small business owners.

This book is about how you can use these new sources of business funding to fill the gaps left by traditional finance. While hundreds of thousands have used the new sources of funding for their business needs, the process to be truly successful isn't well known.

Business owners are still relying on singular sources of funding, paying inflated interest rates or getting nowhere with other sources.

While the traditional model of business funding was to rely on bank loans for financing, the new system is a more strategic process. In the new financing model, you need to take advantage of the benefits within each funding source to grow your business and attain higher amounts of funding from other sources.

It's this staged-model of business financing that can get you from business start-up to millions without the banking connections required for traditional loans.

Stages of Business Funding and Investors

	Early Stage		Expansion Stage		Later Stage
	Seed Funding	Startup Financing	First Stage	Second Stage	Bridge Financing
Investment Need	Validate the business idea through a prototype, market research and testing	Build out the management team and complete product development	Expand production, marketing and sales	Provide working capital for growth	Funding to prepare for initial public offering
Investors	Traditional Loans Peer Loans Incubators		Rewards Crowdfunding	Rewards Crowdfunding Angel & VC Investors Equity Crowdfunding	Investment Banks Equity Crowdfunding

Source: Crowd101

You'll start with easier sources of funding from peer lending and incubators to secure seed and start-up funding. This money will need to be repaid but is easily available and you'll only need it for the first year or two.

Taking your business to the next level will mean tapping the growing market for crowdfunding and equity crowdfunding. Besides business funding, rewards-based crowdfunding offers the potential for viral marketing and building a community around your business. Equity crowdfunding brings the potential to raise millions for your business, expanding sales on an international level.

Building your business through the crowd can attract the big money through angel investors and venture capital groups. We'll cover how to find these investment groups and what they want to see before becoming a part of your success.

The beauty of this new model of staged-financing is that you can stop at any stage, reusing some sources before deciding if latter stages are right for your business. Each chapter includes a real-world example of a business owner that has found success in the funding source.

Being successful in business isn't only about finding the funding to get you started. A solid business plan is crucial to knowing what to expect and finding your competitive advantage in the market. Before jumping into using the new model of funding, you'll learn how to put together a complete plan for your new venture. You'll learn how to avoid the risks in your business strategy before spending any of your own money.

Using these new 'alternative' sources of business funding puts you back in control of your entrepreneurial future. Learn how to tap this four-step process for raising business funding and go from zero to business in no time.

Creating a Business Plan – Making it More than an Idea

Whether you already have a business or just an idea, a business plan is essential. Even if you're not considering raising money for your business, a plan will help you guide your strategy in production, marketing and management.

If you are looking to fund your business, a business plan is a must for building credibility with investors and supporters. Your plan is going to be the first step in developing your idea and the last step before you take your business to investors for funding. Not only will it help you make sure you know what to expect but it will help convince others that you know what you're doing and are ready for the next level.

What to Know before you make a Business Plan

People usually ask me how to make a business plan just as they are getting ready to seek funding for their business idea. Too late!

While a business plan is absolutely necessary for funding, it's also a way to define and refine your business strategy and goals. Writing out a plan forces you to look at everything separately and then how it fits together; from market needs to costs and plans for the future.

The best part about a business plan is that it's a 'living' document. Write out a business plan ahead of your launch to know what you're getting into and set your first year's goals. Revisit your business plan every six months to a year for improvement and reflection.

The Business Plan Life-Cycle

Have you achieved goals? How can the plan change for improvement?

Competitive market analysis and customer needs.

How do you get your product in front of customers?

How does your product fit a niche?

There's no rule to how long you should make a business plan but around 25 to 40 pages plus another ten pages or so for appendices should be enough to get the detail you need.

If a picture is worth a thousand words, a chart or graphic in your business plan is pure gold. Putting as much of your numbers in graphics will break up the monotony of reading, express your best points and cut down on the bulk of your business plan. Investors will appreciate it and it will help you visualize how your business will grow.

Avoid buzzwords and jargon when making your plan. Include any necessary technical notes in an appendix if people want to read them. Most likely, the investors within your sector that know the technical side will not need it and those outside the sector won't want to read it.

Business Plan Essentials

Most business plans contain seven core elements including a one-page executive summary.

Executive Summary – Every business plan starts with an Executive Summary but this part is the last you'll write when working through your plan. The Summary is just one-page of all the most important points from your plan so you'll need to have the rest written to know what goes here

Company description – legal information, employment and funding capital, history plus something like a sales pitch including goals, mission and vision

Products and Services – features and benefits of products or services plus unique selling points that satisfy needs of potential customers

Market Analysis and Strategy– size and growth of potential market, niches within the market, demographics and behaviors of customers, competitor analysis, differentiation in the market, price points and customer expectations

Operations – the plan to physically produce and deliver your product or service to customers, outlining responsibilities of managers, funding needed to start and ongoing expenses

Finances – Financial statements with three to five years of actual data plus up to three years of proforma numbers, funding needs and available credit

Organization and Management – Property and equipment needed, organizational structure, initial staffing needs, and relationships with third-party vendors and suppliers

B-Plan to Do:
- Exec Summary
- Marketing
- Operations
- Finance
-Management

Your Business Plan in Detail

Company description

This first section will include a lot of the legal description for your company like in which state you are based and your legal status. You've got the option of incorporating, forming a partnership or remaining as a sole proprietorship.

- Corporations offer protection of your personal assets against business creditors. If your business runs into trouble, you won't have to worry about losing your home or being personally liable. Corporations can issue stock and may be able to lower the owners' tax bill by holding profits in the company. Corporations generally have stricter filing requirements and must hold an annual meeting of owners. Corporations also must pay corporate income taxes.

- Partnerships and Limited Liability Corporations (LLC) are like a type of corporation but still retain some benefits of a sole proprietorship. There is no limit on the number of owners and the profits flow directly to your individual tax returns, avoiding corporate taxes. There are also no requirements for annual meetings. These business may not be able to issue stock and may have a more difficult time raising investor capital compared to a corporate structure.

- Sole Proprietorship is the easiest business structure to form, basically just starting your business under your own name as the owner. There are no filing requirements as with LLCs or corporations and you won't need to pay corporate income taxes. The downside is that you can be held personally responsible for any business debts and can be sued for something you do as part of your business.

- Non-profit corporations may avoid corporate taxes if the company is approved by your federal revenue service.

The company description will also give a brief history of the business, when it was formed and different business names under which it has operated. Include geographic markets in which you operate, both for production and sales, as well as how many employees work for the company.

You'll wrap the section up with the goals, mission and vision of the company.

- Vision is a statement of what the company wants to be in the future. It is a little more esoteric including a philosophical vision of the ideas and values the company wants to project. It can be as short as a sentence like Nike's, "To be the #1 athletic company in the world," or much longer as with Coca Cola's vision within each idea of profit, people, portfolio, partners and planet.

- Mission is more detailed and specific than a vision statement; describing what the company does, how it operates and for whom it operates. Example: "It is the Mission of Advanced Auto Parts to provide personal vehicle owners and enthusiasts with the vehicle related products and knowledge that fulfill their wants and needs at the right price. Our friendly, knowledgeable and professional staff will help inspire, educate and problem-solve for our customers."

- Goals are still more detailed and direct. What does the company want to accomplish over the next year or several years? Goals usually start with, "To" and are quantifiable. Example: "To become the leading distributor of key chains by market share," or "To improve efficiency and achieve an operating margin of 30% by 2020."

Products and Services

This section lays out your actual product or service as well as the supply chain involved. What raw materials or other supplies do you need? How much manufacturing or finishing is involved in production and how does your product get to the final customer? How many distinct products do you sell and how are they related? What patents or trademarks does the company own or will it need?

This is also where you will talk through the specific needs of your potential customers and how your product satisfies them. Go deeper than just superficial needs to the emotional needs your product fulfills. A luxury fountain pen isn't just a writing instrument, it's a symbol of success and an expression of art in writing.

Spending some time thinking through this section will help you develop your business idea and provide ideas for marketing.

Marketing Research and Strategy

This is where most people jump to when making their business plan. It not only answers the 'why' of overall customer demand and how your product fills a need but how you'll get your product in front of people.

1) Market Research

How big is the market in which you want to sell your product? This is how many people buy the product and how much is spent annually. You could estimate the potential market size if you're creating a totally new product or service but try to relate your new business to an existing market. Even a totally new market will be related to an existing one, most likely a small niche part of the older market.

Try to be as specific as possible in the niche market in which you'll operate.

Niche Example:

1. Entertainment Content
   a. TV Programming
      i. Sports Programming
         1. American Audience
         2. Geographic and Age Targeting

Defining your niche helps to better understand your specific customers and the potential for sales. A new business can't be all things to all people. In the example above, it would be impossible for a new business owner to address all the needs of the general TV-viewing public. Even the behemoth Disney corporation is segmented into different divisions to operate in different areas of entertainment. Investors will want to see a niche market large enough for strong sales but small enough that you can address specific needs.

Are more or less people buying the product and what are sales trends over the last few years? There's nothing wrong with breaking into a declining market but your product will need to be exceptional.

Within your niche, who are your potential customers? Develop a target customer profile including age, income level, family size, marital status, interests and hobbies. What is the buying pattern around your product? Do customers buy it once every few years or more regularly? When a customer needs the product, how urgent is their decision?

What are the legal and regulatory requirements within your market? Don't think that you'll be able to get around state and federal regulations because you're just a small start-up company. Understand filing costs, permits and the inspection process and how much everything will cost.

You will also want to research how regulations are developing within your market. Are product or safety requirements becoming more strict or costly? Is the market heavily regulated but might it be privatized in the future?

What drives purchases for your product or service? These are general factors that will influence how many people buy your product and how many they buy. Is it mostly driven by population growth or some kind of customer demographics? Your growth drivers may be specific to the niche in which you operate. A luxury niche within a larger market will be driven by disposable income growth while the low-cost niche may be driven by other economic factors.

Niche drivers are outside your control and apart from your marketing efforts. It's best to sell into a market with strong and growing drivers that will help push sales for the whole niche.

Example growth drivers for the auto industry:

- Price of gasoline

- Driver preference for types of cars and trucks

- Infrastructure improvement in emerging markets

- Interest rates and loan availability

- Consumer confidence and economic growth

How are products differentiated within the larger market and down through your specific niche market? If products are not differentiated, like the market for agricultural products, then it is a commodity market and you'll have almost no ability to set your own price. Products can be differentiated by brand, extra features or service.

What are the price points for products in the market? Do some companies sell their product for premium prices because of their differentiation? Where will your product fit within the pricing scheme; in the premium segment or the low-cost segment?

Don't immediately think you'll break into your market by offering the absolute lowest price. Existing companies competing on price already have loyal customers and momentum in their marketing strategy. Enter the market at a lower cost and they can just as easily lower their own prices until your profit evaporates.

In my experience, it is usually better to start your business from a position of differentiation than to be a low-cost provider. Market your product as something better with special features relative to existing businesses. Your competitors will have to imitate or improve on your special features to take your customers, something that will be much more difficult compared to just lowering prices.

Competitor research is some of the most productive time you'll spend while developing your business plan. Knowing your competition inside-and-out will help to understand where you fit in the market and if there's really an opportunity or you're heading for disaster.

- How do competitors promote their products?

- Put all your competitors on a scale from most expensive to least expensive price

- How much of the market does each competitor control? Does one competitor dominate the market or are sales spread out more evenly?

- What do your potential customers think about each competitor? Don't just assume this from your own point-of-view, ask them!

- What is each competitor really doing well? How much does it cost them to produce their product? How is each competitor falling short?

Check out Porter's Five Forces, it's a way of looking at competition in your market and is taught in most graduate business schools. Porter's Five Forces separates a market into five aspects (or forces) that influence competition.

Buyer Power – How much choice do customers have to fulfil their need for the product? Do a few customers buy in bulk or are there many customers with smaller orders? Is the customer demand highly subjective to prices or is the product a necessity? If buyers or one particular buyer have a lot of power, then businesses will be limited on how much they can charge and how fast they can raise prices.

Buyers of cable TV services have almost no power because there are so many buyers and single purchases are relatively small. Cable service operators can charge higher prices and change service agreements easily. By comparison, if you are manufacturing agricultural tires then much of your sales are probably to a few large machinery companies and they'll be able to limit your pricing power.

Supplier Power – The flip side of your customers' power is how well do suppliers control the market for inputs. Can you get your resources from one of many suppliers or are you dependent on a few? Do you need one specific item or can you substitute it with something else as an input to your product?

Threat of New Entrants – How easy is it for new competition to enter the market? Are there regulations that limit new competitors or do high start-up costs keep people out? Obviously if there are high barriers to entry, you'll need to address how you plan on getting in the market. Once you're in a market with significant barriers, you might be able to charge higher prices and won't have to spend quite as much on marketing.

Competitive Rivalry – How many competitors are already in the market and do products differ much? Are customers loyal to one brand and does it cost much to switch to another brand? Do companies sell on price competition or quality?

Switching costs can be a huge barrier for new businesses but also a great advantage to have once you're in the market. How long does it take to train staff to use a product or how much would it cost to switch over to a new provider? You have to look at your product from the buyer's perspective. Why are they going to switch to your product once you enter the market?

Threat of Substitution – Do customers need the specific product or can they use something else that will fulfill the same need? How urgent is it that someone buys the product when they first realize the need? Customers of medical products may not buy frequently but they often need a specific product and they need it urgently.

Doing your market research can take months but you will become an expert in the industry. Don't just use one source for your market research and make sure you fact check everything you find on the internet. Detailing your market research within the business plan may seem tedious at times but it will be a key factor to your success and a requirement for getting funding.

Sources of information for market research include:

- Surveys and focus groups – Don't avoid getting information from potential customers and suppliers. It might be more expensive but it will be direct from the people that know.

- Trade magazines and associations – Check out archived journals and annual reports available at your library

- Chamber of Commerce

- Tradeshows and events

- Publicly-traded companies – These companies might be much larger than other competitors but they are required to file reports that will discuss the key issues in the market. Go to the Securities & Exchange Commission (SEC) website and search by company name.

2) Marketing Strategy

Detailing your market research will uncover a lot of opportunities for your product and risks from competition. Once you know how the market functions, you can develop a marketing strategy to take advantage of the opportunities.

Marketing strategy is often separated into the Four Ps: product, price, promotion and place. You've already put together the ideas around your product within market research but you'll need to develop a strategy around the other three.

Promotion is generally the different ways you will market your product and special strategies. Is there seasonality to your product's demand or events around which you can promote? If your product is highly complementary of another product, meaning people usually use the two together, you might want to try promoting it in association. Follow the mailing list of companies selling these complementary products to see when they start promotions. Always have a promotion idea standing by so you can launch it quickly when these complementary products are being promoted.

How and when do your competitors run their promotions? Can you take advantage of massive advertising by competitors to grab customers at the last minute while they're out shopping? If competitors are already spending money to get people to the store, try spending your marketing at the store. Should you run your promotions at the same time as competitors or wait until competitor discounts have finished?

A lot of this will depend on the frequency of customer purchases. You don't want to wait until after your competition is done with promotions if the target customer only buys once a year or occasionally. There may not be many customers left after your competitors' promotions to buy your product.

Place relates to where your customers buy the product, i.e. online, phone or traditional store. Is the product usually sold through a specialty store, a supermarket or a department store?

Besides seasonality in promotions, and whether to do your marketing at the same time as competition, consider promoting at different places in the buying cycle. A potential customer first needs to find out about a product or service. This is usually done through mass market channels like TV or large traffic websites. Then the customer usually needs to go somewhere else to actually buy the product, whether at a store or online.

If your competitor is promoting heavily in the first stage, to increase awareness of the product type, spend your marketing dollars closer to the point of sale. If the customer is going to a physical location like a mall or a store, consider advertising along the most heavily trafficked route or at the store. If the customer usually buys online, promote at more specific websites or where customers generally purchase.

Do you need a dispersed sales force or can a few agents sell the product directly to customers? Will you sell it continuously or do most sales happen sporadically at trade shows and special events? If most of your sales happen sporadically, you might be able to cut down on operating costs by only being a seasonal business.

Price will depend on the market and your own sales strategy. Again, it is usually much better to compete on some differentiation of your product rather than to be the low-cost producer. Being able to sell something for cheaper isn't really much of a special skill and you'll have a tough time convincing investors your business plan is sound.

Is there a gap in existing competitor pricing, i.e. is there a gap between low-cost products and the luxury market? How sensitive to price increases is the customer? Do customers pay attention to prices and is a small increase over competitors' pricing going to be noticed? If one or a few customers have the potential to be big buyers, can you offer a special discount?

Part of your pricing is also going to depend on your own costs and financing needs. Angel and venture capital investors will generally want to see an annual return above 20% for the company. How high do prices need to be to accomplish this return?

Online retail sales are growing at double the rate of traditional store sales. Online sales are expected to grow by 9% a year through 2017 compared to just 4% growth in traditional sales and still have a lot of room to grow.

Forecast: US Online Retail Sales, 2012 To 2017

	2012	2013	2014	2015	2016	2017
(US$ billions)	$231	$262	$291	$319	$345	$370
Year-on-year growth	14%	13%	11%	10%	8%	7%
Share of total retail sales	8%	8%	9%	10%	10%	10%

Source: Forrester Research Online Retail Forecast, 2012 To 2017 (US)

Even if you only sell to a local market, having an online presence can be a huge boost to your business. You'll get the chance to connect with your customers continuously and on a more personal level. You'll also be able to start building an online community around your brand, something that will be essential in one of the funding resources we'll talk about later.

Operations

The operations section of your business plan is going to describe how you plan to physically produce and deliver your product or service to customers. It outlines specific responsibilities of managers, the funding needed to start up operations and ongoing expenses.

Are costs fairly steady from start-up through production or do costs happen more sporadically? You'll develop your funding needs in more detail later in the finance section but you want to tie them directly with operations here. What is the minimum costs to start operations and for the base scenario of sales?

Make sure you cover different scenarios of sales. If you have many more orders than you expect, how quickly can you hire staff and increase production? Are there other suppliers you can go to for bulk ordering and how long does it take to produce the supplies you need for your product?

How long does the supply chain and production process take in your industry? If sales are slower than expected, will there be risk of spoiling or shifts in fashion trends? How deeply will you be able to discount your product to get it out the door?

Financial Statements

From a finance guy's perspective, this section is too often neglected by start-up entrepreneurs. It's great that you've got passion for the idea and a plan for marketing but I want to see how you plan on making money.

Building out your financial statements is not only going to be a requirement for funding but it's going to help give you certainty on your costs and pricing. Too many business owners rush into an idea with only a rough estimate of the costs and then realize there is little or no profit left after they've put their life savings on the line.

Your financials should include at least three statements; the Balance Sheet, Income Statement and the Statement of Cash Flows. These three financial statements track your assets, liabilities, income and cash flow and will be a great exercise in understanding how companies make money in your industry.

Before launching your business, your financial statements will be proforma statements because they are only estimates of the business over the next few years. As a corporation, you'll be required to report the actual results each year though even sole proprietorships will want to track their finances.

When you're ready to seek outside funding, you'll need to include at least two years of actual data along with three to five years of proforma estimates. Larger investors are going to want to see some financial success before they're ready to take a risk but they will also closely scrutinize your estimates for future growth.

The need for that proof of financial success in getting funding is a big part of this book. While more than half a million businesses are started each month, most fail for lack of funding. It's a cruel joke that you need to be successful to get funding from traditional sources but you often need funding to be successful. Using the two alternative sources of funding described later in the book, peer loans and crowdfunding, can help you get over the funding gap that keeps most from achieving their dreams.

Let's take a closer look at each financial statement as well as how to put together your proforma estimates.

The Income Statement

The income statement, also called the Consolidated Statement of Operations, accounts for all sales and expenses over a period of time, usually either a year or a three-month quarter.

An important point is that the income statement does not represent actual cash flow. Sales might be booked well before you get paid if you have a reasonable belief that you'll get the money. Expenses are matched with sales so you might report a cost on the income statement even though if won't be paying it immediately. The idea here is to match the cost of running the business directly with the sales that are generated to show profitability.

Some companies detail out their income statement but the example below will give you a good idea of the concept.

CONSOLIDATED STATEMENTS OF OPERATIONS

	Years ended	
	September 28, 2013	September 29, 2012
Net sales	$170,910	$156,508
Cost of sales	106,606	87,846
Gross margin	64,304	68,662
Operating expenses:		
Research and development	4,475	3,381
Selling, general and administrative	10,830	10,040
Total operating expenses	15,305	13,421
Operating income	48,999	55,241
Other income/(expense), net	1,156	522
Income before provision for income taxes	50,155	55,763
Provision for income taxes	13,118	14,030
Net income	$ 37,037	$ 41,733

Net sales are actually total sales minus any returns. Cost of sales is the cost of all material supplies that go into your product or service.

The gross margin, also shown as a percentage by dividing gross sales by net sales, shows cost profitability of the company.

Your operating expenses are all the costs of running the business and include research, staffing, utilities, office supplies, rents, insurance and marketing. You'll often see much of this in one item called Selling, General & Administrative. For your own financial statements, detail out each cost so you can track your expenses more directly.

An important part of operating expenses is depreciation on your property and equipment. You are allowed to reduce your reported income by the amount of value lost in property and equipment each year. The idea is that you used that equipment to make sales and will eventually need to replace it. While you won't actually see a cash expense for depreciation, it is a very important part of reducing your taxes. Property value is depreciated over 27.5 years while most equipment is depreciated over five years.

The operating income, sales after all operating expenses have been paid, is another important measure of profitability. Your operating margin shows how efficiently you manage costs to create income. You'll want to compare your own profit margin against competitors if public data is available.

Below operating income, you'll deduct for interest paid on debt as well as taxes to get to net income. This is the 'bottom line' and represents your ultimate profitability.

The Balance Sheet

The balance sheet shows your assets, liabilities and equity at a point in time, usually the last day of the reporting period. This is different from the Income Statement and the Statement of Cash Flows which both show activity over the entire period.

Your assets are short-term cash and investments and long-term possessions that can be used to run the business. Liabilities are debt and other obligations that you must pay. Equity is the remainder and represents the value left to the owners of the company.

Balance Sheet for Wal-Mart				
As of Jan 31, 2006				
Assets		**Liabilities and Shareholders' Equity**		
Current Assets:		Current Liabilities:		
Cash and Cash Equivalents	6,414	Commercial Paper		3,754
Receivables	2,662	Accounts Payable		25,373
Inventories	32,191	Accrued Liabilities		13,465
Prepaid Expenses and Other	2,557	Accrued Income Taxes		1,340
Total Current Assets	43,824	Long-term Debt, due within one year		4,595
		Obligations Under Capital Leases, due within one year		299
Property and Equipment, at cost:		Total Current Liabilities		48,826
Land	16,643			
Buildings and Improvements	56,163	Long-term Debt		26,429
Fixtures and Equipment	22,750	Long-term Obligations Under Capital Leases		3,742
Transportation Equipment	1,746	Deferred Income Taxes and Other		4,552
Total Property and Equipment, at cost	97,302	Minority Interest		1,467
Less Accumulated Depreciation	21,427			
Property and Equipment, net	75,875	Shareholders' Equity:		
		Preferred Stock		0
Property Under Capital Lease:	5,578	Common Stock		417
Less Accumulated Amortization	2,163	Capital in Excess of Par Value		2,596
		Accumulated Other Comprehensive Income		1,053
Property Under Capital Lease, net	3,415	Retained Earnings		49,105
Goodwill	12,188			
Other Assets and Deferred Charges	2,885	Total Shareholders' Equity		53,171
Total Assets	138,187	**Total Liabilities and Shareholders' Equity**		138,187

Assets are listed in terms of liquidity, how quickly something can be converted to cash. After cash, receivables are sales you've made on credit and are waiting to be paid. You might see this paired with an 'allowance for bad debts' to account for sales you might not be able to collect.

Inventory is finished products that you haven't sold yet and prepaid expenses are costs for which you've paid up front.

The cost you paid for property and equipment will be offset by the amount of depreciation you've taken on the income statement. This represents the remaining value in the assets but might not actually be the market value or remaining life. You'll also account for the value of patents and goodwill in your long-term assets though most small businesses won't have to worry about them.

Your business liabilities also follow the liquidity format with short-term debts accounted for before long-term debt and lease obligations. Each year, you'll move some of the long-term debt up to the short-term liabilities section to show the amount that comes due within the year.

Right about now, you're probably thinking this is way more accounting than you need. You don't need to be a full-time accountant to successfully run a business but you should know the basic concepts and be able to put together your financial statements even if you never plan on seeking funding.

An introduction to accounting course will give you all the tools you'll need and can really open up the financial side of your business. You're not just doing this for the fun of it, you want to make a profit and most of us can't afford to lose money on a business for very long. Starting with the right tools and an understanding of what kind of profit (if any) is realistic will put you ahead of the vast majority of new business owners.

The Statement of Cash Flows

The statement of cash flows shows actual cash coming in and going out. While the income statement can be manipulated by deferring expenses or moving sales forward, it's much harder for management to change their cash flow numbers. That's why, as an analyst and investor, I spend most of my time reading cash flow statements of potential investments.

Like the income statement, the statement of cash flows shows all activity over the period. It's separated into three sections; cash from operations, investing activities and from financing activities. Your statement of cash flows is constructed entirely from accounting items on the other two statements.

XYZ Company, Inc. Cash Flow Statement For the year ended December 31, 2010 (in thousands)		
		2010
Cash Flows from Operating Activities		
Net Income	$	13,725
Depreciation/Amortization	$	4,000
Changes in other accounts affecting operations:		
(Increase)/decrease in accounts receivable	$	500
(Increase)/decrease in inventories	$	(600)
(Increase)/decrease in prepaid expenses	$	300
Increase/(decrease) in accounts payable	$	(450)
Increase/(decrease) in taxes payable	$	500
Net cash provided by operating activities	$	31,700
Cash Flow from Investing Activities		
Capital expenditures	$	(13,000.00)
Proceeds from sales of equipment	$	-
Proceeds from sales of investments	$	-
Net cash provided by investing activities	$	(13,000.00)
Cash Flow from Financing Activities		
Payments of long-term debt	$	(1,250.00)
Proceeds from issuance of long-term debt	$	500.00
Proceeds from issuance of common stock	$	-
Dividends paid	$	(2,000.00)
Purchase of treasury stock	$	-
Net cash provided by financing activities	$	(2,750.00)
Increase (Decrease) in Cash		15,950.00
Beginning Cash	$	19,050
Ending Cash	$	35,000

Cash from operations is how much cash is generated from the day-to-day business. Since net income does not represent actual cash flow, you have to add back non-cash items that were included on the income statement. This includes depreciation and any changes in working capital. Most of these working capital changes will come from the balance sheet.

The biggest challenge here will be to remember what constitutes a source of cash, and should be added back, or a use of cash and should be deducted.

For example, if you sold more products on credit and increased your accounts receivable then you booked the sale on the income statement but didn't actually collect cash so you need to remove it on the cash flow statement.

Cash flow from investing activities includes any purchases or sales of long-term property or equipment and any money spent on research. Any sales of capital will add to cash while spending will decrease cash. It is common for a normal business to spend cash for investing activities and have a negative number in the total. You want to be growing the business and can't be continuously selling your long-term assets.

Cash flow from financing includes new debt and payment of debt or dividends. If you don't have any stock issued, this section will be relatively small.

The difference in cash over the period will be added or subtracted from the cash you had on the balance sheet in the prior period. The statement of cash flows really ties the whole financial picture together, starting with net income booked and ending with how much cash you have left at the end of the period.

How to put Together a Proforma Income Statement

Whether you are just starting out and don't have actual financial data, or you are seeking funding from investors, you'll need to put together a proforma income statement. You may need to construct proforma estimates for the other two financial statements depending on how much funding you need but an income statement is always required.

A proforma statement is just an estimate for the next two or three years of business. A pre-launch proforma income statement will help you plan costs and profits before getting in over your head. A proforma income statement will also help investors see how their money will grow and what kind of return they can expect.

A proforma income statement looks exactly like a regular statement but is for future years. Even if you're presenting to an investor group for funding, it's important that you be realistic in your estimates and assumptions because analysts like me will question you on everything!

How much in sales can you realistically make over the next couple of years? If you are just starting out, this will come from your estimate of the market size and how much market share you can take from competitors. You might be able to take a percent or less of the market without getting competitors' attention. Don't count on taking much more of the market without a response, either through a price war or heavy marketing, from the competition. How much market share did other new entrants get during their first years? This might be available by looking at annual reports or financial statements of competitors.

Your cost of goods will move along with two factors, price inflation and your sales growth. Is hot market demand for your product increasing the cost of supplies? Will you be able to get discounts for buying in bulk? Increasing this cost of goods number at a slower pace than sales growth is important to show higher profitability but you need to be realistic.

If you are going to be estimating strong sales growth, you better also estimate higher expenses for marketing. I've seen too many business owners come looking for funding, estimating double-digit sales increases but neglecting to estimate how much those sales will cost in terms of marketing. As with many of the estimates, it's best to have an example from another start-up business and how much their expenses increased relative to sales. If you can't find a proxy for your estimates, detail out your marketing expenses with specific costs you will spend on different media and the typical return on marketing costs.

General and administrative costs will be very high for a new business. You'll need at least a small staff, property and equipment just to make any sales. As your sales grow, these costs will need to grow as well but they won't grow at the same rate. Most of the expenses on your income statement can be estimated relative to sales growth, i.e. sales growth increases 20% so administrative costs grow by 15% but it's always best to have some evidence for your estimate.

Don't forget to include estimates for depreciation and interest expense on debt within your proforma income statement. Depreciation will be fairly easy to calculate but interest expense will depend on how much loan funding you plan on taking out.

One of the most commonly missed items on a new business proforma income statement is the carry-forward of losses. If you are losing money after all your expenses, and most new businesses will lose money for at least a year or two, you can carry those loses forward to reduce your taxes in later years. You can carry losses forward for up to seven years, offsetting positive income later to reduce your taxes.

You don't have to be immediately profitable to get investor funding, in fact it might make many investors skeptical of your estimates if you are, but you do need to show that the business is moving in the right direction.

Another valuable use of your financial statements, for your own planning and for funding, will be common-sized financial statement analysis. This is done by taking each line item as a percentage of a common item on each statement.

Shown in the example below, each line on the income statement is shown as a percentage of sales for the year. This helps to show where you are spending the most money in expenses and how that's changing over the years. If there are publicly-traded companies in your industry, this is a great tool to compare your results and to help build estimates of your expenses and profits for the future.

IBM - COMMON SIZE INCOME STATEMENT			
	2010-12	2011-12	2012-12
Revenue	100.00%	100.00%	100.00%
Cost of revenue	53.93%	53.11%	51.87%
Gross profit	46.07%	46.89%	48.13%
Operating expenses			
Research and development	6.03%	5.85%	6.03%
Sales, General and administrative	21.87%	22.07%	22.54%
Total operating expenses	27.90%	27.92%	28.57%
Operating income	18.17%	18.97%	19.56%
Interest Expense	0.37%	0.38%	0.44%
Other income (expense)	1.94%	1.06%	1.83%
Income before taxes	19.75%	19.64%	20.96%
Provision for income taxes	4.90%	4.81%	5.07%
Net income	14.85%	14.83%	15.89%

Source: Morningstar.com

By looking at the example above, we can see that IBM is becoming more profitable and spending a relatively set percentage each year in R&D.

On the balance sheet, you would take each line item as a percentage of total assets. A common-size cash statement analysis isn't done as often as the other two but you would use Cash Flow from Operations as your common divisor.

Short-term working capital

New businesses live and die by their flow of working capital, the short-term money available to buy supplies and pay expenses. There are a few sources of working capital financing that you will need to use effectively. Later-stage investors will also want to see how much working capital financing is available and how efficiently you have used it in the past.

Trade Credit is goods and services used for your product or service for which you don't pay immediately. If you've got a good relationship with suppliers, you might be able to set up a 30- or 60-day payment. The supplier will want proof that you've got orders for your product or service and may want some kind of collateral as security.

Factoring or receivables securitization is another source for short-term financing. When you sell your product or service on credit to a customer, it becomes a receivable on your balance sheet. A factoring company will buy your receivables and may even handle collections. You'll usually have to sell your receivables at a steep discount to how much they're worth depending on the certainty of payment.

Lines of credit are given by banks but not generally for new businesses. If your business has good collateral assets like a building or other property, you might be able to get a line of credit. It's usually at a cheaper rate than other forms of short-term financing and can be revolving each year.

Equity financing isn't really short-term but an important part of funding for new businesses. This is an ownership stake in your company that you sell for funding. It might come from friends, family or someone in your existing personal network.

Organization and Business Structure

New business owners often jump into an idea without thinking through business structure and staffing questions. The smallest sole proprietorship may start in your home office but you have to plan for what you'll need to grow. Are you planning on double- or triple-digit sales growth but not planning on the workload involved?

Even if you are planning on running a one-person show for the next couple of years, it's best to start making the connections you'll need for future growth. Who knows, you may need additional staff sooner than you think.

Start by finding freelancers that can provide ad hoc services when you need them. It can take a while to find quality freelancers so put together a few small projects early to test out a few providers.

Start thinking about what tasks you do regularly that could be outsourced to an assistant. Always balance quality and cost with your work. You may be able to design your own graphics but can an expert do it much faster and at a marginal cost?

You'll also want to write out your relationship with large suppliers and potential alternatives. What happens if your sole provider gets acquired by a competitor or goes out of business? What happens if you get a rush of orders which can't be handled by a current supplier?

When you start seeking funding from investor groups, you'll need to be able to show depth of experience in your management team. If you can demonstrate that people on your management team have been successful in the past, you're much more likely to get and investor's attention. If your core team doesn't have much experience, consider bringing on a few experts as consultants and offering them a limited stake in the company.

Wrapping up the Business Plan – Check and Review

The quality of your market research will be critical to other parts of your business plan so don't skimp on time or money. Double-check all information you get from third-party sources or on the internet and seriously consider doing some of your own research through focus groups and surveys.

Always, always have at least one or two people review your business plan. You're just too close to the material to be able to critique it or find errors. Try getting a review from at least one person outside your team for an independent review.

Your business plan doesn't have to be perfect before you get your business off the ground. Too many entrepreneurs get analysis-paralysis and get bogged down in the details. Put some time into creating your business plan and then get going!

The Truth about Government Small Business Grants

Small business grants are like scholarships and don't have to be paid back so naturally they are the first thing many entrepreneurs think about when looking for startup funding.

The problem is that the myth of free money and government small business grants may not be worth your time. While the government does not technically offer small business grants for most types of businesses, there is a work-around solution but it may still require more time and paperwork than it's worth.

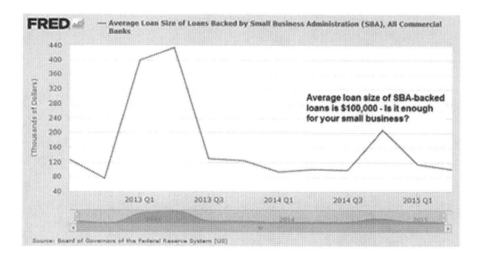

I thought the SBA provided Government Small Business Grants

The myth of easy money through government small business grants and the Small Business Administration (SBA) is pretty common but painfully untrue. The government does not provide grants for starting or expanding a business. The misunderstanding comes from the fact that some grants are available to non-profit organizations and for research and development.

The government does provide small business grants for research in technology. The Small Business Innovation Research (SBIR) offers limited grants to American companies that can further the government's R&D goals. Billion-dollar companies like Symantec, Qualcomm and ViaSat all got started with an SBIR grant but the grants are extremely difficult to get.

There is a work-around to the limited amount of government small business grants but it may still not be the best course for your small business idea. There are some government grants available for non-profit work, available by searching Grants.gov online. These grants are very competitive and generally only available to non-profit organizations. If you can start your company out as a non-profit, developing the idea as a part of a research project that benefits a community, then you might be able to get a government grant.

The problem, besides having to tweak your business model, is that you'll spend quite a bit of time filling out paperwork and there's no guarantee you'll end up getting a grant. The weeks you'll spend searching for and writing up different grant proposals are better spent marketing your business on a grass roots level and using some of the other funding sources we'll talk about in the book.

Rather than spending your time trying to get any government small business grants, you might want to consider one of the six loan programs available through the SBA. There are no fees for loans under $150,000 and loan rates range from about 3% to an 8% cap.

- 7(a) SBA loan program can be used for working capital, revolving funds, equipment purchases and to refinance existing debt. Rates as of August 2015 are set between

5.5% and 8.0% with lower rates for loans paid in less than seven years.

- SBA export-assistance loans are targeted to small businesses that can further America's export competitiveness.

- SBA CDC/504 loans can be used for major purchases of real estate or business equipment. Rates as of August 2015 are set at between 3.6% and 4.4% for terms of 10 or 20 years.

- SBA disaster recovery loans are available to homeowners, businesses and non-profit organizations to repair or replace items damaged or destroyed after a disaster.

- SBA microloans are available for loan needs under $50,000

- SBA express loans are a subset of the 7(a) program with no collateral required for loans under $25,000 but may carry a higher interest rate than the 7(a) program.

What to do if you can't get a SBA Loan

SBA loans carry relatively low interest rates compared to other loans so you'll want to check there first. They are pretty competitive and most businesses are not approved but the SBA representative might still be able to offer some advice on your business plan and point you to other resources.

After an SBA loan, your next stop for funding will be a traditional bank loan but loans under $250,000for small businesses have all but dried up since the financial recession of 2008. Your best bet to get your biz off the ground is going to be through a personal loan or small business peer loan.

How to Use Peer Loans to Jumpstart Your Dream

The traditional system of bank loans and big money investors never really worked that well for most entrepreneurs and has broken down since the financial crisis. Fortunately a whole new system of small business loans and funding has emerged, and it is open to everyone!

Small business loans through peer lending are the first stage in the small business funding process because they are relatively easy to get and can get you to the next level of funding. While rates can be higher than other loans, there are no prepayment penalties and you don't have to sell a portion of the company as in equity financing.

What is Peer Lending for Small Business Loans?

Peer lending is one of the most popular topics on my blog PeerFinance101. The idea couldn't be simpler and is really just the traditional bank lending system brought online, connecting investors directly with borrowers.

It used to be that a business owner would go to the bank for a loan. The bank is in the business of making loans but doesn't necessarily want to hold all their loans so they sell them to an investment firm. The bank gets cash to make more loans, keeps collecting payments and passes the money on to the buyer. The investment firm bundles the loans up and then sells pieces off to investors according to their needs for return, time horizon and other risk factors.

Of course, both the bank and the investment firm take their cut of the profits at each step.

Peer lending takes these middlemen out of the picture. A borrower fills out an application online, either for a personal loan or for a business loan. The peer-to-peer website checks the borrowers credit history and assigns an interest rate. If the borrower accepts the terms, the loan goes live on the site where individual investors can decide to fund it. If the loan is fully-funded, the money is released to the borrower's bank account. They make payments monthly to the website which passes the money on to the investors.

Because there's no bank branch location or profits to be divvied up, investor returns on peer loans are much higher than on traditional bank loans. There is so much investor demand for peer loans right now that almost all loan requests are fully funding in less than a few days.

Some peer lending platforms offer small business loans as well as personal loans. Lending Club offers small business loans up to $300,000 on rates as low as 5.9% for up to five years. The origination fee from 1% to 6% of the loan is paid by the borrower and it will take about a week to complete the process. The time to funding has been another huge advantage of peer loans. Business owners no longer have to worry about losing a prime location or missing payments on working capital.

The table below shows Lending Club small business loans data for the first quarter 2015. Small business loans made up just under 1% of all loans on the site with a quarter of loans on 60-month terms and the rest on 36-month terms.

Lending Club Small Business Loans (Q1 2015)

Rating	Average Loan Amount	Average Rate	Range of Rates
A	$16,413	7.8%	7.0% to 8.2%
B	$14,620	10.8%	8.7% to 12.0%
C	$15,047	13.7%	12.3% to 15.0%
D	$15,214	16.8%	15.6% to 17.9%
E	$17,546	19.7%	18.3% to 22.0%
F	$18,401	24.1%	23.0% to 25.6%
G	$20,341	25.9%	25.8% to 26.1%

Source: Lending Club (data)

It's immediately clear that while small business loans of up to $300k are offered, the vast majority of loans are for much smaller amounts. Loans are unsecured, meaning you don't have to put up collateral, and rates are competitive with most personal loans.

Don't think you have to apply only for a business loan. Personal loans are available for up to $35,000 on terms of three or five years. Personal loans usually require less proof of sales and other metrics compared to business loans.

Why Should You Use Peer Lending First in the Small Business Funding Process?

I wouldn't recommend using a peer loan for continual business funding but it can be a great way to get your company to the next stage in the process.

While crowdfunding can provide funds you don't have to pay back and can offer huge marketing benefits, you'll need some kind of a product or service to offer as rewards. Your small business peer loan can get you the money to develop your idea and build that initial product example. Peer lending is round one of seed funding while the next stage, crowdfunding, will fulfill the rest of your seed funding needs.

Funding for small business loans take as little as a week, much quicker than a traditional bank loan, and can help you take advantage of quick deals on a commercial space or inventory. Peer loans are ideal for business ideas with higher risk, like Matt Griffin's Combat Flip Flops line of footwear manufactured in post-conflict regions.

I interviewed Matt last year after he used a peer loan for buying supplies for his flip flop manufacturing start-up.

Griff's time in Afghanistan opened his eyes to the reality of how economic development can drive education, politics and ultimately peace. It was from this that Combat Flip Flops was born in 2010. Along with co-founders, Donald Lee and Andy Sewrey, the company would manufacture footwear and accessories in post-conflict zones for sale internationally. Besides creating jobs in regions with unemployment as high as 38%, the company also donates a portion of proceeds to local development.

MAKING COOL STUFF IN DANGEROUS PLACES

Our mission is to create peaceful, forward-looking opportunities for self determined entreprenuers affected by conflict. We'll take bold risks to make community connections, create distinct designs, and flip the view on how wars are won.

Learn More>

The company ran into a problem when it went to get materials for the spring line of manufacturing. The flip flops wouldn't be sold until months later but Griff needed to put deposits down for supplies. They tried to go through a traditional bank but lenders wouldn't touch the company because it did business in dangerous locations.

Combat Flip Flops worked through the peer lending platform Street Shares which specializes in veteran-owned businesses. While larger sites like Lending Club and Prosper have more investors that can fund your loan faster, smaller platforms might be able to offer more specialized service. Griff says the team at Street Shares helped the company to build out a loan packet and submit it to the investor network. It took just 20 minutes to put the request together and the loan was fully funded within five days. Griff was able to get the money within two weeks and pay for supplies.

While most peer lending sites set your interest rate before the loan goes to funding, there are some sites that use an auction process where investors bid rates down on loans. Griff's loan funded at a 23% interest rate for $30,000 on a three-year term. The company only needed the funds for 90 days so paid it off early to avoid the interest rate.

Almost all personal loans and peer business loans are originated with no pre-payment penalties. Use a peer loan to get your business started but you might want to use crowdfunding, described in the next chapter, for more funding and to pay off your peer loan early.

Advantages and Disadvantages or Peer Lending for Small Business Loans

Probably the biggest reason to use peer lending for your small business loan is out of necessity. Banks just aren't lending to small businesses anymore. New financial regulations make it just as expensive to originate a $250,000 loan as it is to make larger million-dollar loans, so there's really no profit incentive to make smaller loans.

Recent lending data shows that small business loans have yet to return to levels seen before the Great Recession.

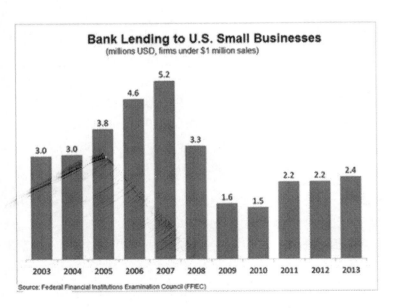

Bank Lending to U.S. Small Businesses
(millions USD, firms under $1 million sales)

Source: Federal Financial Institutions Examination Council (FFIEC)

44

There is so much investor demand for peer lending right now that small business loans are funded quickly. There is no prepayment penalty so take out a three- or five-year loan and pay it off when you can.

A word of warning though, avoid the one-year loans offered by some platforms. They usually charge much higher rates and you'll pay high refinance fees if you can't pay it off.

With peer lending, you don't need to sell a share of the company to investors which probably wouldn't offer much at this stage anyway.

Taking out a small business loan through peer lending also shows backers on your crowdfunding campaign, and later investors, that you are committed to the company. Your loan gives you skin in the game and proves that you believe in the company.

The disadvantage to a peer small business loan is that it must be repaid. Rates can be relatively high compared to secured credit but you shouldn't need to hold the loan for more than a year or two. The next stage in the small business funding process, crowdfunding, may bring enough funding to pay off the remaining principal on your loan.

Realistic Goals for Small Business Loans through Peer Lending

Rates can get prohibitively high for small business loans in the hundreds of thousands so apply for only the minimum amount you need to create a viable product for the next funding stage. Besides your credit score, two things impact the rate on your peer loan. Higher loan amounts and longer-term loans will both increase your rate.

Looking at the small business loan data from Lending Club, rates seem to increase substantially after $20,000 so apply for less than this amount if you can. Use this money to develop your product and some marketing material for your crowdfunding campaign.

It's also helpful if you can give yourself six months before you apply for the loan to improve your credit score. Check your credit reports for any missed payments or errors. If there are errors, you can dispute it with the company and the credit reporting agency to get it wiped off your report. It's not often but it does happen on about 5% of credit reports.

Try paying down the amount of revolving (credit card) debt you have and don't try to get any loans for six months before your peer loan. A soft check of your credit is ok because it won't affect your score but hard inquiries will lower your score and stay on your report. Don't close out any credit accounts and you might even call to get your available credit increased on a few. This will help improve your debt-to-credit ratio, showing that you have lots of credit available and are not scrambling for money. Don't open any new accounts unless you don't have any credit history, just use your existing accounts and pay the bill in full every month. In six months, you'll have a significantly higher score and can get a better rate on a peer loan.

Of course, your ability to repay the loan will also need to be considered. A $15,000 small business loan at 17% on a five-year term will cost about $375 a month. That's workable within most budgets but make sure you have enough to pay the loan even if it takes a while for business sales to begin.

How to Apply for a Peer Loan

Applying for a peer loan for your business or another reason is fairly straight forward and it will usually take less than a week to get your money. We'll run through the process on Lending Club but it's almost identical on other peer lending platforms.

The first thing you see clicking through to the Lending Club website is a small box to add quick information on your loan like amount, loan reason and an estimate of your credit score.

Once you click through, you are taken to a page for personal information before Lending Club can give you a rate for your loan. It is all pretty standard information including name, address and income. None of this affects your credit score.

The approval process takes less than a minute and Lending Club will base your interest rate on your credit score estimate. Rates for borrowers with very good credit scores are extremely low but even the higher interest rates are generally lower than those you'll get on credit cards. This is why loan consolidation accounts for about three-quarters of all Lending Club loans, to pay off high interest credit cards and other loans.

Loan Grade	Interest Rate	Origination Fee	24-Month APR	36-Month APR	60-Month APR
A	5.32% - 7.98%	1% - 4%	6.48% - 9.99%	5.99% - 9.97%	7.02% - 9.63%
B	8.18% - 11.53%	4% - 5%		10.98% - 14.38%	10.38% - 13.80%
C	12.29% - 14.65%	5%		15.90% - 18.31%	14.58% - 16.99%
D	15.61% - 17.86%	5%		19.29% - 21.60%	17.98% - 20.28%
E	18.25% - 20.99%	5%		21.99% - 24.80%	20.68% - 23.49%
F	21.99% - 25.78%	5%		25.82% - 29.70%	24.51% - 28.40%
G	26.77% - 28.99%	5%		30.71% - 32.99%	29.42% - 31.70%

If you agree to the interest rate and think you can manage the monthly payment on the p2p personal loan, clicking through will take you to the final page for personal information. On this page, you are going to enter your contact number, employment status and your social security number.

This is when Lending Club is going to run a hard inquiry on your credit report. The previous check was what is called a soft inquiry and doesn't affect your score. A hard inquiry might lower your credit score for a few months but your loan rate and details won't change.

Once you agree to terms on a Truth in Lending Disclosure Statement, your loan is complete and ready to be funded by investors. Lending Club complies with a pretty extensive review of state and federal regulations where it provides loans so you'll see all the same forms you see in a traditional bank loan.

After your loan is funded, you'll need to verify your identity with Lending Club. This includes verifying your bank account, confirming your email and possibly submitting a few extra documents.

Not all loans need extra docs but you might need to email paystubs or bank statements. These can all be scanned and emailed so it is a fairly easy process. If you don't have these, you can get copies from your work or your bank. The biggest delay in the entire process has been this verification stage so make sure you get your documents sent in as soon as possible.

If you get your docs in and confirm your bank account, loans usually appear in your bank within a couple of days. The whole process can take less than five days for most p2p borrowers.

Lending Club will reduce the amount you get by between 1% to 5% for its origination fee. This depends on the loan grade from A – G but most loans cost the 5% origination fee.

A month after your loan is approved and funded, you'll start making payments. There is no fee for automatic withdrawals from your bank account but Lending Club does charge a $7 fee to process mailed checks.

Lending Club doesn't charge a fee if you pay the loan off early so your p2p loan should be prioritized along with your other debt to pay off quickly. You can make one-time extra payments or just increase the monthly amount you pay on the loan. Make sure you pay your loan on-time every month. Lending Club charges a late fee of $15 if your payment is late by more than 15 days.

Loan Tips to Remember:

- Try for a SBA loan or traditional bank loan first to take advantage of lower rates.

- If you can't get a traditional business loan, take six months to improve your credit score. Use the time to really develop your business idea and get it ready for launch.

- Shop around the peer lending sites for those that offer an auction-style rate process or those that offer the lowest rate on your loan.

- Take out a three-year personal loan or business loan for only the amount you need to get you to the next stage in funding.

- Make regular payments and plan on paying off your loan early with proceeds from the business and your crowdfunding campaign.

Taking your Business to the Crowd

Traditional business funding through loans cost money, lots of money. Peer loans are opening up another source of funding but rates can get prohibitively high on those as well.

Angel investors and private equity investors accept less than a percent of the funding requests they receive. That's 99 out of every 100 businesses that don't get the money they need to grow.

There is a new source of small business funding, one that's providing huge benefits to marketing and customer loyalty beyond the money...

But nobody is using it!

Small business directory Manta sent a poll to its readers before a webinar on crowdfunding. One of the questions was, "Have you ever or would you consider crowdfunding as a source of funds?"

Less than 3% of respondents answered that they had used crowdfunding in the past and less than 15% answered that they would consider raising funds from the new form of financing.

So it comes as a shock to a lot of business owners when I say, "All businesses should be crowdfunding!"

Why every business should be crowdfunding

Let's forget for a moment the potential for business funding from a crowd campaign. That potential for funding is massive. Watch-maker Original Grain has raised more than $390,000 on two products in less than two years. Game-maker Cryptozoic Entertainment regularly raises millions of dollars on Kickstarter for its new games…but put the idea aside for a moment.

The most overlooked reason to crowdfund your business is the opportunity to build an army of customers, and the word army might be more apt than at first glance.

Kickstarter alone gets more than 15 million visitors a month and opening your campaign to social media networks like Facebook and Twitter expands that reach many times over. Your crowdfunding campaign has the potential to take your business national, even international, in an instant.

Crowdfunding backers have an unmatched level of buy-in with the companies they support because they feel like they helped make it happen. Crowdfunding your products turns your customers into something more than just casual buyers, it turns them into soldiers for your mission and they'll help spread the word for as long as you're in business.

Crowdfunding also provides instant validation and development of your product idea.

In the traditional business model, a company would test a product on a small group before rolling it out on a larger scale. The test provides insight into how customers use the product and any problems that might foul things up.

But this kind of product testing is expensive, too expensive for most small businesses. You might be able to test your idea on friends and family but it's unlikely you will have the budget for anything more robust.

Crowdfunding allows you to test your business idea across a massive audience even before production starts. You might still want to create a demo product for trade shows but the feedback you'll get from campaign visitors will be invaluable to tweaking features on the final product.

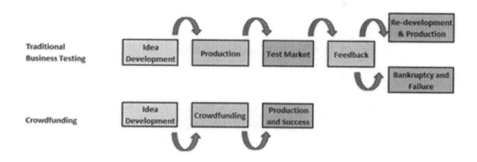

Not only will you get all this information directly from potential customers but you'll get it in real-time. Even traditional product testing takes months to crunch the numbers. With crowdfunding, you'll get messages and emails daily with suggestions for your product.

And acknowledging those suggestions will convert your customers into team members, loyal and eager to promote your business.

The Six Habits of Highly Successful Crowdfunding

Before we get into the process of crowdfunding your business idea, we should talk a little about what to expect in crowdfunding. I get asked the question, "Is my project right for crowdfunding all the time."

The answer is that **every** project is right for crowdfunding but it doesn't mean every person is ready for crowdfunding. Success in business is not really about the project, it's about you and there are six habits that you'll need to work on to be successful.

I call these the **Six Habits of Highly Successful Crowdfunding**.

Personal - Successful crowdfunders share with others and have an active social network. They share their emotions and their excitement. Data shows that campaigns where the founder had just 10 Facebook friends, the odds of making a $10,000 funding goal were just one-in-eleven. For founders with 100 friends, the odds jump to one-in-five.

Comprehensive - People think crowdfunding is simply posting a campaign on Kickstarter and maybe tweeting it out to their network. Crowdfunding is so much more. In fact, I know a lot of small business owners that have completely revamped their marketing strategy around crowdfunding. An effective crowdfunding campaign involves offline and online marketing, strategic management, logistics, research and outreach. You'll need a comprehensive plan to bring everything together.

Team Builder - Effective crowdfunding means building a team to help you reach your goal. While the project may be your brain-child, realize that it has the potential to be bigger than yourself, and will benefit from a team effort. One of the biggest surprises crowdfunders run into is the amount of time a campaign can take. The outreach, networking and general administration you will need to do while your campaign is live can easily take 20 hours or more each week.

Slava Rubin, founder of Indiegogo, states that teams raise an average of 70% more money than campaigns run by a single person. Putting together a team of your most passionate supporters helps in two ways. It will bring expertise and skills from the experience of your team and will spread some of the work around so you're not run ragged.

Aggressive - Only your mother is going to help your crowdfunding campaign without being asked. If you are not ready to ask people for help, sometimes asking more than once, then you need to rethink whether crowdfunding is for you.

According to the Public Management Institute, not asking is the single biggest mistake in fundraising. Only about half (56%) of households say they have been asked to give to at least one non-profit, of these, 95% said they gave to at least one.

Creative - There are nearly 8,500 projects live right now on Kickstarter alone. A great product will not sell itself and you need to get creative to get people's attention.

About 30% of supporters on Kickstarter are repeat backers, who regularly support multiple campaigns. Asked how they decide which campaigns to support; 27% said they support campaigns that make them laugh, 15% support campaigns that make them think, 42% support campaigns with cool products and 16% support campaigns that evoke other emotions.

Strategic - So much media attention goes to crowdfunding success stories that people don't realize how much goes into an effective crowdfunding campaign. Crowdfunding is not writing out a few words and waiting a couple of months for your campaign to end. You'll need to put together a complete strategy from outreach and building your online presence to the logistics behind fulfilling your reward promises.

Campaigns that raise no money before their launch have an average success rate of just 15 percent. For campaigns that raise just 5% of their goal before launch, the success rate jumps to 50 percent.

Pre-Launch Crowdfunding

Now we start getting into the real process of raising money in the crowd and leveraging your campaign for all the benefits to your business.

If you think crowdfunding is about putting together a quick page on Kickstarter and then waiting for the crowd to take over, you're not alone. But you would also not be alone when your campaign was part of the 60% that fail to reach its funding goal.

Success in crowdfunding is all about the pre-launch, the excitement and community you build over the months leading up to your campaign. In fact, 11 of the 17 steps in my crowdfunding book, Step-by-Step Crowdfunding, are in the pre-launch stage.

Follow the pre-launch process correctly and the support for your business will be more than you imagined possible.

Shaping a Successful Crowdfunding Idea

A crowdfunding campaign is a page launched on one of the platforms like Kickstarter or Indiegogo where a project owner pitches a product or cause for backing. The page includes a brief video, the pitch for why the project should be funded, a budget, timeline and a series of 'rewards' that backers will receive for their donation.

The beauty of crowdfunding for business is that backers are not receiving rewards for a donation, they are buying products and becoming customers. I know business owners that crowdfund each new product they develop. The rewards can include other products, branded merchandise and the crowdfunded product with different features.

Launching your new product as a crowdfunding campaign turns Kickstarter into an extension of your own website, an extension with international credibility and millions of visitors a month!

Think of crowdfunding more as a marketing campaign than a funding resource and you'll start to see that raising money is the least of the benefits.

Crowdfunding campaigns are generally live for 30- to 45-days with a successful pre-launch campaign lasting two or three months ahead of time. Depending on how long production and order fulfillment takes, your timeline may extend for several months after the campaign.

Developing your pre-launch campaign idea starts with building a team. For a small business owner, this means assigning an employee to the campaign. For a business idea, it might mean recruiting from friends, family and your personal network.

From your conversations with friends and family, you should be able to get at least one or two people that are interested enough to commit a little extra time to be involved. This doesn't have to mean a big commitment but can be as little as spending an hour or two each week to answer emails or perform outreach tasks. Have a few easy tasks in mind to suggest, or talk with them about what they would be best able to do and when.

The idea of recruiting from friends and family first is two-fold. You'll be starting from the level of trust and friendship which will help in securing some kind of commitment. You'll also get the opportunity to practice bringing people closer into the community of your crowdfunding campaign. This practice is going to be important as you start asking for higher levels of commitment from people that may not know you as well.

How Much Will Your Crowdfunding Idea Cost?

For small businesses, much of your crowdfunding costs will come from your marketing budget and the cost of an employee to manage the campaign. You can run a crowdfunding campaign on almost no budget at all if you do everything yourself but it might not be practical if you have a business to run at the same time.

Creating a detailed budget for your campaign will go a long way to establish trust and credibility with your supporters. It shows that you're not just a random campaign asking for money but a legitimate business with something to offer.

Within your budget spreadsheet, you will start with the basic expenses:

- Marketing expenses - Will you need to advertise what your project or business offers? We'll cover different ways to market your campaign later but most will be identical to general small business marketing.

- Administrative expenses – Most of your admin expenses will be around time spent on the campaign and around the product itself rather than with the crowdfunding campaign.

  o A lot of the admin expense depends on how big you want your business to get. Are you going to need a formal office space or can you make due from existing space? No one expects you to run your business out of the garage forever. Even Mark Zuckerberg had to move Facebook out of his dorm room eventually.

○ Professional fees -The crowdfunding idea and campaign might have been your brainchild, but no one expects you to be all things. If you haven't used professional services in your business yet, you might want to consider graphic designers, videographers, and outreach specialists for your campaign.

Rewards, the products you plan on exchanging for campaign donations, and the cost of delivering those rewards are an integral part of your budget. This is where the budgeting can get a little tricky though because you might not know exactly how many of each reward-level will be chosen.

Figure out how much it will cost to produce each reward, remembering that you might be able to get volume discounts if you produce in large quantities. Don't forget to add in an approximate cost for shipping each within the United States.

Once you know how much it will cost to produce and ship each reward, you can go one of two routes for a basic idea of rewards fulfillment.

• You can assume that an equal amount of your funding is spread across each reward-level. If you are raising $10,000 and have five reward levels, then each one will bring $2,000 in pledges. From here, you divide the $2,000 into the reward size to find how many of that reward you would need to produce and deliver. Do this across all reward levels and you will get an idea of how much everything will cost.

• A safer method is to assume that all your funding comes at the most expensive reward level. You will take the expenses from producing and delivering the necessary amount of rewards at that level against your funding goal. I like this method because it gives you a worst-case estimate for cost of rewards fulfillment.

Your crowdfunding campaign will be seen as an extension of your business profits by the Internal Revenue Service and taxed as such. You can offset the money you raise through all the costs of the campaign and production but need to keep track of these for bookkeeping.

After you have selected the crowdfunding platform most appropriate for your campaign, you will have an idea of fees charged to raise the money. Most platforms charge around 5% of the money raised and around 3% for processing the funds. For example, if you need to raise $1,000 to cover expenses, then you will need to set your crowdfunding goal at $1,087 to have $1,000 left over after the 8% fees.

Setting your crowdfunding goal

Once you have a rough idea for how much your product will cost to launch, you need to make one of the most important decisions in crowdfunding.

Too many crowdfunding campaigns reach for tens of thousands of dollars or more to fund years' worth of expenses or the whole production process. The business owner puts in countless hours towards the campaign only to miss the funding goal and receive nothing in the all-or-nothing Kickstarter model.

Instead of trying to fund everything with just one campaign, consider setting your funding goal high enough to reach a milestone like a test product or a draft copy. Nearly three-fourths of Kickstarter campaigns raise less than $10,000 and less than 3% raise more than $100,000 successfully.

Established businesses generally raise more than the average but it's best to set the mark low for your first campaign.

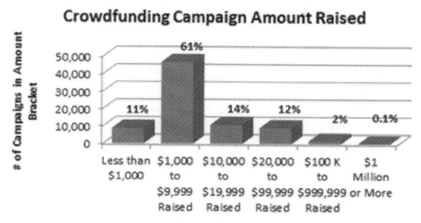

Source: Kickstarter Stats, 2014

My advice would be to set the bar low for your initial crowdfunding campaign, only trying to raise enough that you can provide a working model or something as a reward to backers. With a successful campaign under your belt, it will be much easier to fund successive campaigns since you will already have a base of backers and experience as a guide.

Setting a Timeline for your Crowdfunding Idea

The final step in putting together your crowdfunding idea is to develop a basic timeline for the project. Some of this will depend on your own deadlines and circumstances but there are a few rules you should remember.

I generally recommend pre-launching a campaign for at least three months if you are just starting your business idea. If you've already been selling products and have a customer base, you can probably get along with two months of pre-launching.

Studies have shown that shorter campaigns are relatively more effective than longer ones. This is because visitors to your crowdfunding page get a sense of urgency if they see that the campaign is coming to a close within a few weeks. If your campaign has more than 30 days left, some of that urgency is lost and there is no guarantee that visitors will come back later and support your project.

Budgeting rewards and fulfillment should give you an idea of how long it will take for delivery. Talk to your suppliers about contingencies for higher quantities of production if you end up blowing away your funding goal. Plan out three different scenarios for production costs and fulfillment times, then take the average of the three as an estimate.

Once you have an estimate for how long it will take to produce and deliver awards, a good rule of thumb is to increase this amount of time by 20 percent. There is nothing wrong with delivering rewards ahead of schedule but you really do not want to fall behind.

Knowing about how long your crowdfunding campaign will take from pre-launch through rewards fulfillment can help to build in a really important idea into the schedule. Try planning your crowdfunding campaign to coincide with a conference or other industry event. Getting a booth or just having a demo product on-hand is a great way to showcase your idea and get people to visit your crowdfunding page. Conferences represent a major source of potential backers that you know will be interested in your product.

I've included an example graphic for a crowdfunding timeline below. I assumed general times I've seen in successful campaigns including:

- Shaping an idea (3 weeks)

- Campaign research (2 weeks)

- Campaign outreach (3 weeks)

- Community building (9 weeks)

- Revising the campaign and write-up (1 week)

- Running the campaign (6 weeks)

- Post-campaign fulfillment (5 weeks)

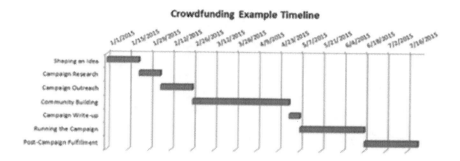

Researching your crowdfunding campaign

Researching a crowdfunding campaign is usually an after-thought for most in their crowdfunding campaign strategy but can help keep you from avoiding the mistakes that keep nearly two-thirds of crowdfunding campaigns from reaching their goal.

Assuming you know what you want to crowdfund, your first step is to find out how that type of crowdfunding campaign does on different platforms. The best way to do this is to look for previous campaigns that related to your idea.

The idea is to find at least a few successful projects and a few unsuccessful projects that are very similar to your own. You're going to study these campaigns.

- How much were they trying to raise?

- How many backers did they eventually get and how much did each pledge on average?

- What rewards did they offer?

- How did their video look?

- Were they effective in sharing their passion for the product or cause?

- How did they connect with people on an emotional level?

- Did they lay out their budget and timeline clearly?

- Do they have a website or blog for the crowdfunding campaign?

The easiest course is just to contact the campaign owner directly. I've had pretty good success with this in the past, getting replies from a little over half of prior campaigns. You'll be surprised how willing people are to talk and help out, especially if your campaign is related to theirs.

- Check out Kicktraq for the project or ask the campaign owner if they have any analytics they could share. Kicktraq is an online tool for seeing daily progress in a crowdfunding campaign's funding and seeing what worked in promotions.

- What forums or groups did the campaign owner get involved with to promote the project? Where any particularly effective?

- You might want to develop a relationship over a few calls or emails but you might even be able to get a list of backers or people that were really passionate about the campaign.

Kicktraq graph of a Crowdfunding Campaign

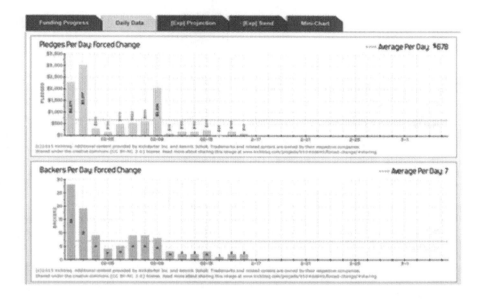

The update and comments section of a crowdfunding campaign page can give you a lot of great information about how the campaign was going and how owners dealt with the progress. Beyond going right to the campaign owner, this is the best place to get tips on campaigns similar to yours.

Once you're done researching previous crowdfunding campaigns, you should have a pretty good idea of what you're up against with your own campaign. You'll know specific challenges to the type of campaign and how well it is received on social media. You should also have a good start on your outreach list for influencers and others passionate about your crowdfunding campaign topic.

Setting Realistic Crowdfunding Goals

The most common questions I get from crowdfunding campaigns are, "How much can I raise?" and, "How do I set realistic crowdfunding goals?" While there are no hard-and-fast rules for every campaign, there are some good rules of thumb to follow to help make your crowdfunding campaign a success.

Once you've budgeted out all your expenses, I would normally recommend you increase it by 10% for miscellaneous expenses and surprises. Crowdfunding is hard enough but running out of money before you fulfill your campaign promises will make it even harder to raise any more money in follow-up campaigns.

After you've put together a detailed budget for your project, it's time for a reality check. Sure, the Star Citizen video game campaign raised $2.1 million but what are your chances?

There are two important tips when deciding how high to set your crowdfunding campaign goal:

- If possible, try an initial campaign where you just raise money for idea development. Raise money for market research, legal filings and development of a prototype. This will give you a much lower target at which to aim and will be easier to fund. You'll also have a successful campaign to show potential supporters in follow-up campaigns and you will learn a ton about what it takes to run a successful crowdfunding project.

- Let your pre-launch success help determine your crowdfunding campaign goal. Campaigns that raise no money before their launch have an average success rate of just 15 percent. For campaigns that raise 5% of their goal, the success rate jumps to 50 percent. Try raising money for a month before the campaign. Then set your funding goal at less than 10 times the amount you raised pre-launch. That means you'll already have at least 10% of your funding goal raised when you launch.

Crowdfunding Rewards Basics

Crowdfunding rewards are not really rewards in the sense that you are giving something away in a contest. Crowdfunding rewards are more like products, services and special recognition you sell in exchange for people contributing to your campaign.

Crowdfunding rewards at the lower levels are going to be trivial items like a thank you, a t-shirt or a digital copy of your work. Making the reward levels cumulative, meaning that each level earns the previous rewards as well, can help incentivize people to contribute to one higher level than they might otherwise.

In a study of more than 200 campaigns, I found campaigns with as few as three rewards and as many as 20 reward levels. Three is way too few reward levels but you also don't need as many as twenty. The average across all the campaigns was 12 reward levels with a median of nine levels.

The more creative you can get with your crowdfunding rewards, the more you will interest random visitors to your crowdfunding campaign page.

- Contributions of $10 or less will get a personalized thank you by email or snail mail.

- Contributions of between $10 and $25 may get a digital version of the work or an invitation to a special event.

- Contributions of between $25 and $50 will generally get some kind of physical product along with prior rewards.

- Contributions of $100 or more might get special recognition on the work, multiple copies of the work to use as gifts or even an interview or lunch with the campaign owner or cast.

While you may be crowdfunding a product for your business, try getting creative with your rewards. Partnering with a social cause or organization can really open up your campaign to more backers and show your support of the community.

Beyond a basic rewards strategy, you'll want to consider the ideas below to boost your campaign.

Limited time or quantity crowdfunding rewards are a good way to build on that sense of urgency within crowdfunding. The most often used of these is limited quantity rewards, giving backers an early-bird offer to get some of the most sought after rewards. Limited-time rewards work best after you've built out a list of backers and community so you can email out the offer.

Add-on crowdfunding rewards is an upsell idea you can pitch to current backers and can be a great way towards the end of the campaign to get that last bit of funding to put you over your goal. The idea is that you contact your current backer list or even your outreach list and offer an add-on reward for backers of a certain reward level. The idea works best if it is for a limited time as well.

While it may not necessarily be a reward, promoting **a limited-time backer pledge** is a powerful way to reinvigorate your campaign. You first need to find a few backers or a new donor that is willing to offer a special reward or match pledge for a limited time. You then promote the match pledge or reward out through current backers and through social networks - Today only! 100% Matching on All Pledges!

My favorite crowdfunding rewards strategy is the stretch goal. The idea is that you set an initial funding goal that is well within reach but will still allow you to develop your product or idea, and then make a set of progressively higher funding goals that will allow you to do extra things for your idea.

Game-maker Cryptozoic Entertainment has worked stretch goals perfectly and raised more than seven-times their funding goals in two Kickstarter crowdfunding campaigns.

Each stretch funding goal is well within reach of the previous one and includes a special incentive or reward. The game-maker builds a lot of enthusiasm around each successive goal by introducing a new game character and a whole story behind it. This helps drive multiple pledges from backers and gives them a reason to share the campaign with their network.

Outreach for your crowdfunding campaign

A lot of the outreach for your crowdfunding campaign will be similar to marketing and outreach of your business.

It's during outreach that you are going to make the initial connections with potential backers, cheerleaders and the all-important influencer.

- Outreach starts with a simple introduction and building out your list of people that might be interested in the campaign. For established businesses, this starts with your customer list and the people that visit your store on a regular basis.

- Start with smaller requests like advice and social shares of your blog posts to bring people into the campaign and build a sense of community. Crowdfunding is about building a community around your brand. Use it for this intent first and people will be more than willing to donate later.

- Don't think that support starts and stops with financial backing. Get to know the people on your outreach list to understand where they can help the most. Offering multiple opportunities to support the campaign will make it easier for them than simply asking for financial support or nothing

While researching previous campaigns can give you a ton of information around which to design your own crowdfunding campaign, it can also provide one of the best ready-made outreach networks. Previous crowdfunding campaign owners have already built their network and searched for the best places for their online presence.

If you did not contact previous campaign owners in your crowdfunding research, you'll want to do it now. **If you are shy about reaching out and talking to strangers, forget about crowdfunding.** Only your mother is going to help your campaign without asking. Most others will have to be asked and sometimes asked multiple times.

- Did they find any social groups on Facebook or LinkedIn that is related to the topic and yielded some good interest from members?

- Did they find any online forums or websites that were particularly helpful?

- Did they find any blogs or bloggers that were receptive to guest posts or talking about the campaign?

- Did they find any journalists or publications that were interested in hearing about the campaign?

Social media can be extremely frustrating for crowdfunding campaigns. While everyone knows it's a pipe dream, there is still that little voice in the back of your head that says, "Maybe my campaign will go viral." After spending tens of hours crafting a social media strategy, low social shares of your campaign can be unbearable.

Understand that click-through rates, or the percentage of recipients that open and click on a link, for email are between 1% and 5% depending on your industry. The rate for social media is even lower, around 0.4% to 0.8% for Facebook and Twitter. Even if people share your post on their social profile, they may not click through and actually look at the campaign.

Before you get too discouraged, there are ways to improve the response to your social media posts. It begins with finding the people that are most likely to share your posts in the first place, those affinity groups that share a passion for the topic or product.

In **Facebook**, you will look for group pages. An important distinction here is to be made between a group and a page. Facebook pages are like personal profiles but for a business or organization. Your crowdfunding campaign should have its own page. Facebook groups are an affinity groups set up for communication around the common interest but not necessarily a common organization.

As with other outreach groups, try out a few Facebook groups to get the feel for how helpful each might be. A lot of groups will degenerate into worthless spamming if the moderators are not present. Find a couple of groups where people share valuable insight and opinions and start building your presence.

With your group participation, it isn't about reaching everyone in the group but building a relationship with a few members. Since these people are already passionate about the topic, they are likely to be part of a wider social network around the idea and more willing to help you with the campaign.

Twitter does not offer a group function but you can create lists that will work in a similar way. When you tweet, you can tweet only to the list or to your general profile page. You can also decide if list members' tweets go to your general page or only to the list. There isn't the same sense of community in Twitter lists but it does provide a way of separating the tweets into specific groups.

- Click on the Lists tab on your profile page and create a list.

- You can add people to your list, share a list with others and request to be added to lists.

- Through the tweets you see from people on topic-related lists, make a note of common hashtags and other Twitter profiles.

Journalist and traditional media contacts are like the Holy Grail for crowdfunding. Getting your campaign on the news or in a widely published periodical can mean tens of thousands in donations and a viral campaign.

There are two things to remember for getting journalists to cover your campaign, the story and who is most likely to want it.

Your first step is researching which journalists or publications are most likely to be interested in your story. This is usually fairly simple and just a matter of noting the journalists that frequently write about a topic. After all your other research into your campaign, you will likely have come across at least a few names that keep popping up. Even if your campaign is not locally-focused, you will want to note which local journalists cover the topic as well.

The second part of getting journalist coverage is creating a story that others will want to hear. The best way to do this is by partnering with a social cause or relating the campaign to the community.

Once you've developed your story and found journalists that might be interested, contact them through a brief email or a press release. You may have to follow up a few times and don't be surprised if you only receive a few responses. You only need one shot at media attention to really boost your campaign.

Drawing people to your crowdfunding campaign

I am going to assume you have a website for your business and some kind of blog page on the site. If you don't have these, you really need to consider starting your online presence. Even posting once a week to your blog will start to build your name as an expert and start sending you traffic from Google search.

Think you don't need a website because your business is all local? That's when a website is most important. Since your website and blog will be locally-focused, it will be much easier to start showing up in local Google searches. It's your best chance at cornering your local market.

Once you've got a website, you can use the same ideas below to drive visitors to your site as well as your crowdfunding campaign.

Guest Posting is writing posts for other bloggers to use on their site. What?! It takes long enough to write stuff for my own blog, why am I going to just give it away to someone else?

Because what is the point of writing posts if no one is there to read them? Other bloggers already have visitors that come by every day. They already have built up their blog's search rankings and get lots of traffic from Google. Writing a guest post for a highly-trafficked blog is like hanging a sign out for your business in front of Walmart.

Here is how the process works:

- During the research phase of your crowdfunding pre-launch activities, you are going to be finding other blogs that relate to your crowdfunding campaign. They might be blogs that share the same social cause or cater to people that are interested in a certain product, say tech gadgets.

- Bloggers constantly get emails asking if they will allow a guest post or promote someone's blog. You can't just spam out an email and expect a result. Build up a relationship with these bloggers by reading their blog and posting comments. Ask them for advice on your own blog, your crowdfunding campaign or on your product.

- Propose at least three topics on which you might write about when you contact the blogger. These should be topics that will interest their readers but also have something to do with your business and crowdfunding campaign.

- If you don't hear back from someone, send a friendly reminder in a week but don't be pushy. If they answer positively then thank them and make sure you write a strong, informative article. You will want to include one link to your website and another link to your crowdfunding campaign page.

- I've guest posted on blogs that were scheduled out more than six weeks so you will want to get started on this early if you want to get posts published before your crowdfunding campaign launch.

Guest blogging works on several levels. First, it establishes your name as an expert on a subject and actually reaches an audience.

Guest blogging is also important for your website's ranking in search engines. Google sees that another blog, maybe a blog that ranks highly for a keyword or topic, provides a link to your website. Google uses this to assume that your blog must be important for that topic as well. Build up enough links to your business website from other quality sites and your own website will start showing up higher in search as well.

Social media is actually a surprisingly small portion of the visitor traffic to most established blogs but is a bigger help for crowdfunding campaigns. It helps if you've spent some time building a real relationship with the people on social networks. Adding a bunch of acquaintances doesn't mean they are going to actively support your business or crowdfunding campaign.

Some people spend a lot of time on social media but you'll want to focus your crowdfunding campaign blog on three sites: Facebook, Twitter and LinkedIn.

- Do I even need to talk about **Facebook**? With more than 1.3 billion visitors, the site is pretty much obligatory for everyone. You should have a Facebook page for your business and a personal page for yourself. Pasting the URL website address of your blog posts into the updates box on your Facebook business page will generate a link and image from the post. You will want to share your business posts on your own personal page and within relevant groups but don't just spam it out everywhere. Do this for at least a couple of months to build a following for your business before launching your crowdfunding campaign.

- Don't make the common mistake and think that your entire social media strategy is simply reposting your blog posts on the social networks. Social media is a two-way street; otherwise, it wouldn't be social. Sharing other people's posts will help put you on their radar for a guest post or link in the future and will provide valuable content to your followers. You'll also want to ask and answer questions to build that truly social relationship.

- **Twitter** is another social network, but your posts are limited to 140 characters. These tweets can be everything from updating followers on what you're doing or how you're feeling to tweeting out a link to new developments at your business.

- **LinkedIn** is like Facebook for professionals and business. Beyond professional profiles, the network is a great source for groups where you can connect with other business owners and people interested in your industry. The important thing to remember with LinkedIn is to keep it professional. You are not going to be posting pictures of your cat in the sweater you knitted.

Wrapping up your crowdfunding pre-launch

There are just a few more ideas you might want to consider before actually launching the crowdfunding campaign for your business.

Probably the most fun you'll have with your crowdfunding campaign is the launch party. Even if your crowdfunding campaign isn't local in nature, getting 50 people together to talk about the campaign and get excited about the launch can give it a life of its own.

Leading up to the launch, but at least a month in advance, start talking to email subscribers about the idea of a launch party. This should give you an idea about how many might be interested. You'll want to talk to some of your most passionate supporters about helping out with the party, maybe reaching out to their high-profile contacts or friends in the press.

You don't have to go Kardashian with the budget. If you can bring in a large group of people, you shouldn't have too hard a time partnering with a local establishment. One crowdfunding campaign hosted their launch party at a local bar with the campaign owners serving as bartenders for a few hours during the night. In exchange for the crowd, the bar helped pay for marketing the event and discounted drinks.

It helps to have at least two or three people that can act as fire-starters at the launch party, people that share your passion for the campaign and are not shy about spreading their excitement. You and your team of fire-starters should meet up before the party to put together talking points and ideas.

Your goal is going to be to raise 20% of your crowdfunding campaign goal at the launch party. Take a page from non-profits and set up a movable goal-board to track your progress. Backers do not have to offer a live donation at the event but can write a pledge card and go to the campaign page when it goes live. Raising 20% or more of your crowdfunding goal within the first couple of days gives you a better chance of being featured by the crowdfunding platform as a hot campaign.

Turn supporters into cheerleaders and team-members before the campaign. A crowdfunding campaign can be a lot of work and you've got a business to run. Rally a few of your supporters to help out while the campaign is live.

First, you need to know your supporters and customers personally. You should aim to do this as a way to make your business personal anyway but it will also give you a chance to understand how to use their strengths for more than financial support.

Some of your supporters may be natural marketers or good business planners. Do any of them have experience in video or photography production? Can they write for your blog or post on another blog? Do they have any media or internet contacts that might help the campaign go viral?

Even getting your supporters to pass your crowdfunding campaign page or blog through their social network can help bring hundreds of new people to the cause. You have to ask though and you might have to ask a couple of times. There's no room for the shyness in business or crowdfunding.

Starting your Campaign the Right Way

So you've spent months pre-launching your crowdfunding campaign, creating your outreach list and building a community around the campaign. You have a strong team around the project that is just as passionate about it as you are and you've ironed out all the wrinkles in the idea.

Now what?

Now you're actually ready to start crowdfunding! You are ready to put your campaign down on a platform and launch the project.

The actual pieces of your campaign page will be slightly different depending on which platform you choose. I will describe the process for a Kickstarter page below but most of the ideas will be generalizable across any platform. Opening an account on any of the sites is pretty easy, just putting in some personal information and choosing your screen name.

While the campaign title should be something catchy and interesting, you want to use your real name or business name as the creator of the project. For the creator's image, choose a picture of yourself that will show up clearly in a very small size. This is so your friends and family will easily recognize the campaign as yours when they visit the page.

Shorter campaigns create more sense of urgency while longer campaigns give you more time to raise money. Generally, campaigns of 30 to 45 days work best and should be all you need if you've already put in the time pre-launching the idea. Most campaigns start and end strong but fizzle out during the middle period. This can lead to terrific disappointment and cause you to lose faith and motivation. It's best to set a shorter campaign to minimize the cursed mid-campaign period and keep a greater sense of urgency on backers.

Make sure you plan your crowdfunding schedule so that your campaign does not end on a holiday or a weekend. Most campaigns see their best support over the last few days. It's best to have people around their computers to see your outreach and marketing. It will likely take the platform staff a couple of days to approve the campaign so plan accordingly.

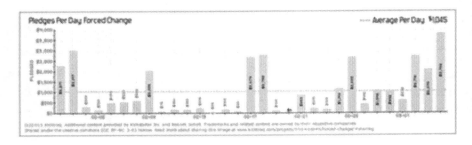

Parts of the Crowdfunding Page

While you want your campaign title to be relevant to the product, there's nothing wrong with spicing it up a little. Most campaigns use their product name followed by a colon (:) and then some kind of interesting descriptive. You might try your slogan if it is interesting or descriptive enough to grab someone's attention. Spend a little time brainstorming at least three or four titles and then run them by someone on the team.

Next, choose around ten images that really show the product from a visual perspective. These images should speak to the need your product satisfies for customers or fans. The best image will be your cover and the rest will be used throughout the campaign page.

Immediately following your video on the page should be your 30-second elevator pitch. Written down, this will probably be about two short paragraphs. For many people that visit your page, this may be as far down as they read and it's your only chance to convert casual internet surfers to backers.

Your pitch needs four elements:

- What's in it for me? – As a business campaign, most people will be looking at your product and the rewards offered. Partnering with a non-profit organization or cause helps to extend this to an emotional level.

- Urgency - People need to understand why they should care and why your campaign needs supported NOW! Build in limited-time rewards and your business funding needs.

- The ask! Don't forget to actually tell people how they can make a difference and ask for them to join the community around your campaign. Don't just ask people to become backers, ask them to reach out to you and be a part of the team.

If your elevator pitch did its job, then people are primed to read a longer description of your campaign. Consider a strong image after the pitch and then lead into the full description of your campaign.

Be honest and conversational in your campaign page. Crowdfunding is first and foremost a social tool and people want to be reached on a personal level. Talking in the first person, using pronouns like I, you and me will help make this connection.

Include links to your website in the bio and link all your social network sites into the campaign page. Don't forget to ask people to click through and be a part of the community on your Twitter, Facebook and your other social network profiles.

You should itemize your budget but keep it conversational. Talk about how much it will cost for major budget items and how important they are for the project. Listing out your budget and talking through it will help build credibility and prove that you've thought the project through completely.

Finally, you will want to talk through a realistic timeline for the campaign. Include a brief summary of everything you did during the pre-launch of the campaign to show people just how hard you've worked on the project.

Once you've got your campaign page written out, let it set for at least a day. Have one or two other people look it over and provide feedback. If you submit your campaign for review immediately after having written it up, you are much less likely to catch any mistakes. After you've let it sit for a day and gotten feedback from others on the team, read through it and see if there's room for improvement.

After submitting your page for review to the crowdfunding platform staff, you'll need to review it again and agree to the platform's terms before it goes live.

Marketing your crowdfunding campaign

The last section we'll cover here in crowdfunding is how to market your campaign. A lot of these ideas will apply to your general business marketing while some may be more specific to crowdfunding.

Spending your time on free methods of pre-launch crowdfunding marketing will get you the most bang for your buck but there are still some great ways to get free and inexpensive marketing for your crowdfunding campaign after it has gone live.

Despite the fact that crowdfunding is an online phenomenon, offline outreach and marketing is still a very effective tool.

If you didn't throw a crowdfunding pre-launch party, you need to host one as soon as possible after the launch. Even if you did host a pre-launch, consider hosting another party towards the end of the campaign. After a few weeks of crowdfunding, you should know enough new people to build interest in another event.

Of all the crowdfunding marketing events or advertising you do, the event branded around your own campaign will be the most effective at helping you meet your funding goal. People are there to talk about and be sold on your campaign. Even if they just wanted to get out of the house, there will be that feeling of obligation to at least listen to your pitch. As with the pre-launch, gather a team of enthusiastic supporters before the party to build your strategy:

- Key talking points around the campaign

- What does the campaign mean for different people?

- How to ask for a pledge and how to handle common rejection excuses

- How to ask for non-monetary support like outreach to a group or professional services

Next to the campaign party, conferences and trade shows are the next best thing to a targeted audience. I have talked to campaigns that funded their entire goal from one conference, simply by having a demo model that people could try out. This is why I recommend planning your campaign dates around a large event. After really seeing your product, people can immediately go to the campaign page to lock in their pledge.

Your budget may not allow for booth space but you can still carry a demo model of your product around with you. Without the focus of a formal booth, you will need to actively approach people to talk about your campaign.

- Lead in with your 30-second pitch.

- Ask questions and genuinely get to know who they are and their business or personal needs.

- Ask if you can show them your product or service.

- Emphasize how it is applicable to something you heard them mention.

- Aggressively ask for their support on the campaign and ask for a specific reward level.

- Offer to show them the campaign page on their tablet or phone or offer to open the page on yours.

- Get their business card.

Online Crowdfunding Marketing

The problem with online marketing is a terrifically-low click through rate (CTR) on advertising. Research from Coull.com shows a CTR of just 0.1% for display ads. That means 1,000 people will need to see your ad before one person clicks through to the target.

Social media click-through rates are not much better. Rates on Facebook were 0.5% to 2% while ads on Twitter were as high as three percent. The performance of Twitter ads may be short-lived and it's expected that, as more ads are placed on the site, the effectiveness will fall in line with other media.

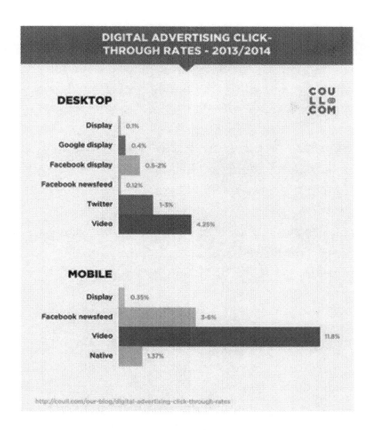

In fact, each one of us sees about 1,700 banner ads each month. Do you remember any of them?

So the question becomes, "How to advertise online without throwing money at it?"

Don't Just Make One Video

Looking at the graphic on advertising effectiveness, the answer to the question should be fairly obvious. Click through rates on video advertising are consistently higher than any other form and as high as 12% on mobile.

Of the different places to spend money on your campaign, video production should be one of the top on your list. You do not need a Hollywood saga but should spend a little for production and editing. The use of video can really take your campaign and business beyond script and evoke the emotion you need to build community.

Fortunately, video production is one of those things that gets much cheaper in bulk. Getting the professional out to your site may cost a few hundred but once he's out there it may only be a marginal expense to shoot several different scenes. Take advantage of this and draw up at least three videos, each no more than two or three minutes long. You'll need one as your main campaign video but the others can be used to really bring out the story.

For your additional videos:

- **Make it a series.** If you can craft a compelling story and then split it across the series, you might get some serious buy-in as people come back to see successive videos. Your product or service may determine the mood but get creative. Your series does not have to be a factual commercial but could be a thriller-comedy-action saga where your product just happens to feature prominently.

- **Cover different needs or emotions with each.** If you've got several really good selling points to your campaign but they get lost when all included at once, focus on each through a separate video. Odds are better that one of your messages will resonate with viewers.

Beyond the obvious places to upload your video series, there are a couple more that may surprise you. Of course, YouTube should be your first stop followed by Vimeo and Vevo. The three offer paid packages but you should only need the free features.

Beyond images, Flickr is also gaining popularity as a video-hosting site and boasts 16.5 million unique visitors a month. Don't forget to post your videos and share across Facebook as well. The fact that videos are not yet as prevalent across these two sites will help yours stand out and drive traffic back to the crowdfunding campaign.

A Rewards-Crowdfunding Example

I interviewed Dan Muszynski during his $10,000 campaign on Indiegogo. Dan founded All Crumbs Bakery in Toledo, Ohio several years earlier but had not yet found the money for a storefront location. He was selling through farmers' markets and wholesale to local restaurants but thought that having an actual store could really boost sales.

He struggled with the idea of asking people for money and help but quickly realized that crowdfunding was about more than asking for a handout. The $10,000 needed for a retail storefront and more equipment could really help take his business to the next level and start giving back to the community.

Besides offering some of the bakery's breads and baked goods as rewards to campaign supporters, Dan did something a lot of crowdfunders are doing to help build community for the campaign. He partnered with a local non-profit organization to deliver loaves of bread to those in need and built it into the crowdfunding rewards.

Through the 123 supporters of the campaign, 14 people signed up to become customers of the bakery's twelve-months baked goods package and 16 signed up for the Cookie of the Month club. These are long-term customers that will continue to support the bakery for years.

The All Crumbs Campaign didn't reach its $10,000 goal but was using the flexible-funding model on Indiegogo and collected over

$6,000 for its retail space. The money was enough to get started and the company donated 1,200 loaves of bread to the local Food for Thought food pantry. The goodwill and loyal customers gained from the crowdfunding campaign has helped to keep the business going strong ever since.

Leveraging your campaign success for business success

The time it takes to put together and manage a successful crowdfunding campaign around your business means you really need to use it for every potential benefit.

Make sure you, or someone on your staff, is actively engaging the online community with messages during the campaign. Crowdfunding supporters get buyer's remorse as well and you need to constantly reassure people that the campaign is for a good product or cause and that their involvement is appreciated.

Once you've raised your money and closed out the campaign, keep this communication going. Thank your supporters for being a part of the team and keep them updated on the timeline for rewards fulfillment.

The most successful businesses build on their previous crowdfunding success with new campaigns and new products. Your second and third campaigns will be immeasurably easier than the first and can potentially raise much more money.

You may end up doing so well with rewards-based crowdfunding that you won't need to seek other funding sources.

Crowdfunding Tips to Remember:

- Don't overlook the non-monetary benefits of crowdfunding your business idea. Every business should try crowdfunding a project even if it doesn't need the money.

- Spend at least two months pre-launching your crowdfunding campaign, building support and developing your idea.

- Make your customers and contributors part of the team. It not only means more help for your campaign but will turn them into loyal cheerleaders rather than just casual customers.

- Leverage your crowdfunding success by keeping a blog going after the campaign and building enthusiasm for the next campaign.

Finding an Angel for your Small Business

Crowdfunding has truly opened up small business funding but it's still developing and you may still need the old school methods to raise enough money to really take your business to the next level.

While alternative finance like peer lending and crowdfunding is emerging as a strong source for business funding, angel groups and venture capital (VC) money is still the dream resource for most businesses.

Angel investors and venture capital firms each funded about $30 billion in deals last year, according to the industry's HALO report. These investment firms seek out early stage companies that need money for growth but they provide much more than just startup capital.

Getting a piece of that money isn't easy though. Angel investor groups may agree to talk with one out of ten of the pitches they receive and may only fund one out of ten of those. Learn what angel investors and venture capital firms want and how to pitch them to get your slice of the pie.

What are Angel Investors?

Angel investors are usually wealthy individuals that form groups to pool their money and invest in very early-stage companies. Angel groups might have upwards of 100 members with each investing a small amount per deal. If you've seen the "reality" show Shark Tank, it is a little like that but much more professional and less scripted. In the 2014 HALO report, angel-funded companies were valued around $3 million before the investment with an average investment of $1.6 million.

Most Active Angel Groups
Total Deals 2014 (descending order)
- Houston Angel Network
- Tech Coast Angels
- Desert Angels
- Launchpad Venture Group
- New York Angels
- Golden Seeds
- Central Texas Angel Network
- Maine Angels
- Wisconsin Investment Partners
- Baylor Angel Network
- Atlanta Technology Angels
- Keiretsu Forum

Source: Angel Resource Institute (HALO Report)

Venture capital firms are investment companies that collect money from many wealthy investors and are run by a general partner. VC firms generally invest much more in a company, averaging more than $5 million per deal.

Angel investors generally make local and sector-specific investments compared to venture capital firms that may invest in a wider range of companies. Angel groups are usually comprised of people that have been extremely successful in a specific sector like technology or healthcare. They invest exclusively in businesses within the sector and generally within their region of the country.

Angel investor groups will usually invest in earlier-stage businesses than venture capital. Angel groups may invest once a company is ready to do a test version of the product while VC groups usually want to see results from early market sales or a test product.

Just like crowdfunding, a lot of business owners think of angel investors as simply a source of funding. The money is nice but only part of the benefit from getting an investment from an angel group. Since angel investors generally invest in a specific sector, they have all the experience and connections you'll need to succeed. In fact, one of the requirements to receiving angel or venture money will usually be that you allow the group to help guide the business.

Is Angel or VC Investment Right for My Business?

After reading through this chapter, you'll need to do a reality check on your business and whether you want to seek funding from an angel or VC group. While the two sources can provide a lifetime of experience and take your business to the next level, beyond the millions they'll provide in funding, most businesses are never going to get in the door of an angel or VC firm.

Not approaching angel funding doesn't mean you can't be successful or can't still raise millions for your business. We'll look at equity crowdfunding in the next chapter as an alternative to angel funding, one that can provide benefits beyond those you'll see from professional investment groups.

You may not want to sell some of the ownership rights to your company, at any price. Rewards-based crowdfunding can be used as many times as you like to raise as much money as you need and build your community.

The point of the whole book has been to understand your options for business funding. Understanding your options doesn't mean you have to use each one. Understanding which sources of funding you've got a realistic chance at getting, besides how and when to apply, will save you years of fumbling through applications and sales pitches.

There are upwards of 301,000 angel and VC groups in the United States. Deal sizes vary but average just under $3.5 million which means just over 8,500 companies are funded. Compare that to the millions of new businesses started each year and you start to get a picture of how competitive it is to get angel funding.

Answer the seven questions below on a scale of one to 10, with 0 being a flat no and 10 meaning you are 100% sure the answer is yes.

1) **Do you have proprietary technology or a unique service?** Have you developed some hardware or software that nobody knows about? Is there nobody else in the extended market doing anything like what you're planning?

2) **Can you take market share of at least 3% from the competition?** If you're going to be competing against large, established companies like Walmart and Amazon, forget about angel funding. Investment groups like to see little or no competition in your potential market but will settle for small competitors that aren't well established. If your business creates a new market from an older one, you might get someone's attention. If it merely improves on an existing service or product, you might need to seek funding elsewhere.

3) **How realistic is your business plan and distribution plan?** You may have a great idea but how well have you thought about production, marketing and getting it to your

customers? Have you spent any time doing real market research to see how eager customers will be for the new product or service? If you are creating a new market, will you need to educate consumers about the opportunity first?

4) **What is the profit margin and level of support needed for your product?** Angel and VC investors will want to see that you are able to make at least 20% profit on your product or service, and likely much higher depending on the industry. This means realistically planning out all expenses pre- and post-sale to show how much your business can make. Too much post-sale support needed can kill a deal unless customers are willing to pay for ongoing support.

5) **Is the potential market at least $150 million in annual sales?** Investor groups want to see the potential for huge sales even if you are only able to grab a few percentage points of the market. That means selling into a potential market of at least $150 million or more.

6) **Does your management team have prior experience and the skills necessary to succeed?** Management should have more than a few years of experience and some real success stories from previous roles. Sure, Mark Zuckerberg started from his dorm room but he's by far the exception.

7) **How committed are you to the company?** How much have the founders, management team and other investors put into the company? Investor groups want to see funding from others as a way of social proof for the business. This usually means prior funding well into the hundreds of thousands of dollars.

Answering from zero to ten on each question means a max score of 70 points. If you can honestly say your business scores around 50 or higher on this test, you might be a good candidate for angel or VC funding.

Beyond the overall scoring, there are some questions that you must score at least an eight to be an angel or VC candidate. Market size (5), management experience (6) and market share (2) will be extremely important to investment groups. Without a high level of confidence in these three, investors will just not have enough certainty to fund your project.

What do Angel Investors want to see in your startup?

Angel investors and venture capital firms are in it for the money. Big shock, I know.

While there is a social component for angel investors, the underlying goal is still to make money on their business investments.

Angel investors and VC firms will generally want to see a return of five-times on their investment over five years. If they invest $1 million for 20% of the company, valuing the company at $5 million, they want to see an estimate that the company will be worth approximately $25 million in five years. This would allow them to cash out for $5 million or five-times their investment.

Valuing your company's potential can be difficult because it depends on a lot of estimates. How fast will you be able to grow sales each year and past the five-year mark? How big is the potential market and how much market share can you take in sales?

Why do they require this high of a return? More than half of their investments in startups are likely to go bankrupt and a few others will probably just break even by the end of five years. Angel investors need to make 20% to 30% a year on the few investments that actually work out.

Besides the money, there's also a social component in angel investing. Angel investor groups usually have it within their mission statement to support and help develop their specific sector. They still want to make money but it's an added bonus if they can help make the world a better place at the same time.

Angel Investor Investments by Sector

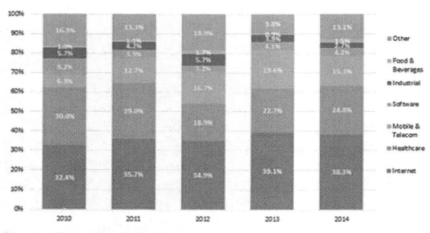

Yearly Share of Angel Group Dollars by Sector
Internet & Healthcare Alone Account for 63% of Invested Capital

Source: Angel Resource Institute (HALO Report)

How to get angel investors excited about your startup?

Your chance at that $30 billion in angel investor money starts with your business plan. We covered the business plan earlier but it's important to repeat a few key ideas you'll need to show investors.

- **How is your business unique and competitive?** You don't have to reinvent the wheel but you better be able to show that your wheel can go much faster or further than any other.

- **What is the total market size for your product and how much share can you grab in five years?** The total sales for your product or service should be at least $100 million or you better have a strong plan to take significant market share. Remember, angel investors need to see five-times their return on what will be an investment of at least a few hundred thousand dollars.

- **How much funding will you need in the next five years?** Angel investors and venture capital firms are usually willing to make multiple investments but they want to know exactly how much you'll need over their investment period. Will you need money to mass produce your product after an initial stage of testing?

- **What will the profits be on the business?** You should have a very good idea of how much it will cost to produce your product, manage the business and the price at which you can sell it.

- **How strong is your management team?** They say success in business is 1% inspiration and 99% perspiration, and no one knows this better than angel investors. They will want to see that people on your team have been successful before or have significant experience in the sector.

Most small business entrepreneurs are not finance people and the pro-forma statement is usually where they get the door slammed in their faces. Pro-forma statements are your financial statements;

income, balance sheet and cash flows, for the current year and estimating out over the next five years. These statements are what you use to show how much money the company can make and how much it will be worth at the end of the period.

Putting a credible pro-forma statement together means having someone on the team that knows financial statements. An angel group will want to see all the assumptions and estimates you used to build your financial statements, and they better be realistic.

PROFORMA INCOME STATEMENT	2008	2009	2010	2011	2012
Revenue					
Distribution Solutions	2,025.00	2,314.00	2,552.00	2,775.00	3,257.00
Technology Solutions	2,984.00	3,064.00	3,124.00	3,195.00	3,310.00
Total Revenue	5,009.00	5,378.00	5,676.00	5,970.00	6,567.00
Cost of Revenues					
Cost of Sales	0.00	0.00	0.00	0.00	0.00
Total Cost of Revenues	0.00	0.00	0.00	0.00	0.00
Gross Income	5,009.00	5,378.00	5,676.00	5,970.00	6,567.00
Gross Margin (%)	100.0%	100.0%	100.0%	100.0%	100.0%
SG&A Expense	3,065.00	3,192.00	3,164.00	3,390.00	3,689.00
Research & Development Expenses	347.00	364.00	376.00	407.00	440.00
Restructuring & Other cash charges (Gains)	0.00	0.00	0.00	0.00	0.00
Other Operating Expenses (Gains)	(5.00)	493.00	(20.00)	213.00	149.00
(EBITDA)	1,602.00	1,329.00	2,156.00	1,960.00	2,289.00
(EBITDA Margin)	32.0%	24.7%	38.0%	32.8%	34.9%
Depreciation & Amortization	124.00	133.00	148.00	139.00	140.00
Total Operating Expense	3,531.00	4,182.00	3,668.00	4,149.00	4,418.00
Operating Income (EBIT)	1,478.00	1,196.00	2,008.00	1,821.00	2,149.00
Operating Income Margin (EBIT Margin)	29.5%	22.2%	35.4%	30.5%	32.7%
Interest Expense (Income)	142.00	144.00	187.00	222.00	251.00
Interest & Other Income (Expense)	121.00	12.00	43.00	36.00	21.00
Interest & Investment Expense (Income)	21.00	132.00	144.00	186.00	230.00
Net Income Before Taxes (EBT)	1,457.00	1,064.00	1,864.00	1,635.00	1,919.00
Provision for Income Taxes (Benefit)	468.00	241.00	601.00	505.00	516.00
Effective Tax Rate	32.1%	22.7%	32.2%	30.9%	26.9%
Net Income from Continuing Operations	989.00	823.00	1,263.00	1,130.00	1,403.00
Income from Discontinued Operations, After-Tax Non-Recurring (Items), Accounting	1.00	0.00	0.00	(72.00)	0.00
(Preferred Dividends)	0.00	0.00	0.00	0.00	0.00
Net Income (E)	988.00	823.00	1,263.00	1,202.00	1,403.00
SHARES OUTSTANDING					
Total Common Shares Outstanding	277.000	271.000	271.000	252.000	235.000
Basic Weighted Average Shares	291.000	275.000	269.000	258.500	246.000
Diluted Weighted Average Shares	298.000	279.000	273.200	263.300	251.000
EARNINGS PER SHARE					
Basic EPS	3.40	2.99	4.70	4.65	5.70
Diluted EPS	3.32	2.95	4.62	4.57	5.59
Basic EPS - Continuing Operations	3.40	2.99	4.70	4.37	5.70
Diluted EPS - Continuing Operations	3.32	2.95	4.62	4.29	5.59
Dividend per Common Share	0.24	0.48	0.48	0.72	0.80

If you are able to get a foot in the door with an angel investor group, then you will need to give a 20- or 40-minute presentation. Leave the touchy-feely corporate video at home. Your presentation must be direct and demonstrate a real advantage over the competition. After your presentation, you'll likely get another half hour or more of questions from the group.

You must know the minimum amount of money that you'll be happy with and have a negotiating plan. Just because you are asking for $1 million for 10% of your company doesn't mean the angel investors are going to see it that way. Be ready to walk away from the table rather than accept a deal with which you won't be happy later. You will need to work with the investor group for upwards of five years if you accept their money, you better be on good terms.

Before pitching the investor group, you will want to consult with a patent lawyer and protect your intellectual property. A lot of entrepreneurs put off this expense but you are going to need to pay it eventually.

Where can you find Angel Investors?

There are more than 300,000 angel investor groups and just under 1,000 venture capital funds in North America. It usually isn't too difficult to find groups in your area or within your sector. You'll find directories at the websites linked below and will likely have a few ideas if your business is big enough to need this type of funding.

Angel Investor Deals by Region

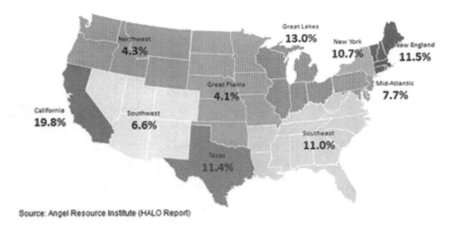

Great Lakes
13.0%

New York
10.7%

New England
11.5%

Northwest
4.3%

Great Plains
4.1%

Mid-Atlantic
7.7%

California
19.8%

Southwest
6.6%

Southeast
11.0%

Texas
11.4%

Source: Angel Resource Institute (HALO Report)

Start with the three organizations below to build your contacts within your area. You'll also want to ask around your local Chamber of Commerce and any business groups in the area. Search through your contacts on LinkedIn to find people in your network that might be able to make an introduction to someone closer to an investment group. Personal introductions will go a long way to getting your foot in the door for a presentation.

AngelList

Angel Capital Association

National Venture Capital Association

A word of warning, avoid any funding brokers that promise to get you investor funding for an upfront fee. Anyone asking for money upfront is likely running a broker scam. There are funding brokers out there but they only represent businesses in which they believe in enough to work on a commission or ownership position.

Before signing on with a funding broker, ask to see a list of companies they've funded and reach out to the businesses. Do a little research and make sure they are legitimate businesses and not just friends of the broker. Make sure you hire your own lawyer to check through all documents the funding broker provides and check to make sure the deal still makes sense after the broker's commission is taken out.

The real trick is getting your foot in the door with any of these funds to present your case for business funding. Once you've found a few angel investor groups or venture capital firms that might be interested in your business, ask yourself these three questions:

- **What other companies have they funded?** Angel groups and VC firms generally invest in the same types of companies. This may also help uncover some contacts for an introduction.

- **Do you have any business relationships or potential relationships with funded companies?** Investors like it when companies in their investment portfolio can help each other out. It increases the chance that both will be successful. Your chances increase if you can bring something to the table that will help another funded company through their business relationship with your company.

- **What legal or accounting firms does the angel or VC group use?** Knowing someone at these legal or accounting firms can help uncover contacts for an introduction and give you an idea on the profits the angel group wants to see in your presentation.

After finding a few targets, you will need to get a personal introduction to the angel group or the VC firm. Send your proposal through the standard channels or a broker and you're not likely to get in the door.

Along with the personal introduction, you will want to provide an executive summary of your business plan, no longer than a few pages, and your pro-forma financial statements. If the angel group likes what they see, they will grant you a meeting where you can present your full business plan and presentation.

Along with your executive summary, you should have a copy of your references available listing out clients, vendors, business associates and contacts that can vouch for your abilities. These people should have direct experience with you and know your prior successes.

If you are able to get the group's attention, you'll first sit through a detailed investment review with one of the firm's analysts, either on the phone or in-person. The analyst will go over your entire business plan, focusing on the proforma financial statements. If you know any equity analysts, it's a good idea to sit down and do a mock review to understand what you will face. Be ready to answer questions on all your financial assumptions and show how you estimated your numbers.

How to Network your Way to Angel Funding

A few tips on networking your way to an introduction with an angel group will go a long way. The most important thing to remember is to be patient and methodical. You are not going to come out of nowhere and get a personal introduction overnight. You need a plan for how you will build trust with your existing network or with new connections and then how to work that into an introduction to an angel investor.

Networking events of professional organizations are a good start. These can be within your industry, banking groups or general business professionals' groups. If you are going to be attending networking events within your industry, try to find out who will be in attendance and the major players in the supply chain. Things get awkward when you find yourself talking to the owner of a major competitor after you've given your 15-second pitch.

Don't be shy at networking events. People are there to meet others and it's perfectly acceptable to approach total strangers and strike up a conversation. Be ready to make a little small talk first about the event or the organization. The question, "What do you do?" will come up quickly so be ready with a very brief 15-second response. You're not trying to pitch everyone you meet, you just want to make an impression so they remember what you're doing.

Don't forget to actually listen to other people and make it a point to remember names and what they are doing as well. Networking is a two-way street and much more a process than most people understand. You won't build enough trust with someone from one chance encounter to get an introduction through their network. The relationship will need to be nurtured through questions, social media and other communication.

It helps to have a process in mind for building relationships. After the networking event, give it a couple of days and reach out to some of the most promising connections. Ask a question or comment on something they mentioned at the event. Mention you saw them on LinkedIn or within a Facebook group and ask to connect. From there, you can keep the conversation going once or twice a week.

LinkedIn is a great tool for finding connections you need to get funding. By searching through your connections, you can find people that will be able to connect you with angel investors or VC groups. Understand that a lot of the connections on LinkedIn are little more than acquaintances so do a little research to see how closely two people are connected. Do they comment on each other's posts? Are they connected on more than one social network?

Partners in the supply chain are a great place to start networking. These are businesses supplying the raw materials for your product or distribution for your product. Your success could mean their success as well and they can offer a lot of information on how to succeed in the industry. Don't talk about your competitors or any trade secrets unless you are extremely close friends.

Do not...DO NOT be that guy at networking events! Don't eat or drink to extremes. You are not there for a free meal or to get drunk. Have a bite to eat if it's offered and one drink but don't use alcohol as a crutch to start conversations.

Using VC Forums to Practice your Pitch

A great resource for practicing and refining the investment case for your business is through VC and other investment forums. These are usually one- or two-day conferences or events where funding seekers are allowed to pitch their businesses.

These conferences may charge a fee for attendance but will include workshops and seminars, as well as networking opportunities. You'll likely have to pitch the conference administrators first or at least fill out an application for your pitch.

If selected, you'll usually have between five and 15 minutes to make your investment case so you may have to shorten your formal presentation to just cover the highlights.

The idea is not as much to land funding at the conference but to get input from the audience, improve your pitch and make a few contacts. Be honest and upfront about any problems you're having with your business plan or presentation. People will be willing to help and might be able to offer suggestions or introduce you to someone that can help.

Call forum administrators to get an idea of how many investors and how many service providers will be in attendance. It's always best to have a high number of investor groups relative to small businesses. Ask how many people are expected to apply to give a presentation and how many presentations will be given.

Don't kill your deal with Angel Investors

That's the general process for finding angel investors for your small business idea but there are a few more points to consider. Remember the points below to avoid some of the most common mistakes entrepreneurs make with angel investors.

- Have a clear exit strategy – Angel investors want to see how their investment works out at the end of five years. They want to know that you are willing to be acquired or sell their share of the business to another investor. This will involve either selling shares to the general public through an IPO, selling or merging the company or producing enough cash to buy out the investor group.

- Have a clearly defined market and a unique selling proposition – Angel investors don't generally want to see that you are tackling a huge global market all at once. Have a plan to conquer your niche market and how your product has unique advantages over existing competitors.

- Have a market large enough to support the investment – Unless you're able to dominate the market in five years, which is very unlikely for a startup, your small market share needs to be enough to validate the investment criteria. Work through the amount for which you're asking, the amount of sales you expect in year five and the return you expect on the angel funds.

- Be ready to listen and accept constructive criticism – Angel investors need to make sure you are ready to accept their help in your business. They will grill you with questions and criticism after your presentation to see how well you accept their ideas.

- Use reasonable assumptions for your pro-forma statements – It's tempting to be optimistic on the potential for your business idea but angel investors know the sector very well and they will be able to see through unrealistic estimates.

After your Initial Presentation

After all that work, after you've given your presentation and the angel group likes what they've heard, you're still not done. The angel or VC group is going to have a process of vetting the idea before they carry through with their investment.

The angel or VC group will do a Due Diligence investigation on your company. This involves a detailed review and research of your business plan, financial accounts and legal structure.

They will look into any previous and pending contracts as well as do a full background check on all executives of the management team. The background check will include credit reports, criminal and legal proceedings as well as a securities check with the Securities & Exchange Commission (SEC) and the National Association of Securities Dealers (NASD).

Any issues that come up in due diligence that weren't disclosed could quickly kill your deal. If the investor group doesn't find anything that cannot be resolved, they will provide a term sheet outlining the conditions and rights under which the group will invest in your business. The term sheet will include an initial valuation of the company, the percentage ownership the investor group will require according to a funding amount, the voting rights and management control the group will require.

Angel Funding Tips to Remember:

- You'll first need to decide if angel or VC funding is right for your business or worth your time to approach. Is your business growing fast enough to even attract investor money? Do you want to sell an ownership position for a slice of a bigger pie?

- The key to an angel group presentation is a personal introduction and a rock-solid presentation.

- Practice your presentation and financials several times with someone in the investment analysis business, preferably someone with prior experience with private company deals.

- Work on your personal relationship with someone that can connect you to an angel group. Don't just contact an acquaintance out of the blue and expect their support.

- Consider attending a venture capital forum to learn more about how the process works and which investment groups are active in your area.

How to Use Equity Crowdfunding for Small Business Funding

Equity crowdfunding is the third or fourth stage in our business funding process, either used before or instead of funding from Angel Investors. Equity crowdfunding your small business can help you raise millions to take your business from the early stages of development through to national and even international sales.

Being able to secure funding from a large group of investors, along with the growth that follows, can also help get the attention of angel investors for a chance at higher funding amounts.

What is Equity Crowdfunding?

Angel investors and venture capital firms invest in as little as two or three deals out of 100 presentations and only allow a small percentage of small businesses to make a pitch in the first place.

To provide another avenue for small business funding, the government passed the 506(c) exemption to the Securities Act of 1933. The exemption, part of the Jumpstart our Business Startups (JOBS) Act of 2012, allows businesses to raise money online from accredited investors through equity crowdfunding. These regulations have recently been expanded to allow funding from any investor.

In the past, a company looking to raise money through selling stock would first go to an investment bank. This investment firm would help refine all the financial documents and fill out regulatory requirements for listing on the stock exchanges. The investment bank then goes on a 'road show', typically taking someone from the company along, to visit large investor groups. This road show is to pre-sell shares of the company and build support for when the company issues shares in their initial public offering (IPO).

Equity crowdfunding is a lot like issuing shares of ownership in the stock market. You list your funding campaign on one of the online platforms like EquityNet or Crowdfunder, providing financial projections and regulatory documents. You reach out to investor groups and individual investors to invest in the company, much as an investment bank would reach out to investors to sell your stock issuance. In exchange business funding, you sell an ownership portion of the company to investors. Equity crowdfunding can also raise money through debt issuance, receiving business loans from investors in the crowd.

Equity crowdfunding as a funding source is still working its way through Washington and there are a few types with different rules. Under the most common 506(c), you can raise unlimited funds but only from investors with a certain level of income and net worth. Under two other types of equity crowdfunding, you can only raise up to $50 million a year but can do so from any investors.

Equity Crowdfunding Regulations

	Regulation A (Tier 1)	Regulation A (Tier 2)	Regulation D 506(c)
Max Funding	$20,000,000	$50,000,000	Unlimited
Investors	Any	Any	Only Accredited Investors
Investment Limits	None	$2,000 minimum with no more than 5% of net worth or 10% of net worth for high-income investors	None
Shareholder Limits	None	None but with conditions	2,000
Investor Income Verification	None	Self-Certification by Investor	Business must verify
SEC Approval	SEC and State Approval required	SEC approval required	None
Financial Disclosures	Audited Financials	Audited Financials	None
Regular Filings	None	Annual and Semi-annual	None

Source: Securities and Exchange Commission (SEC)
This chart should not be construed as legal counsel. Regulatory requirements change and issuers should check for the most updated requirements.

Equity crowdfunding is different from the more popular rewards-based crowdfunding on sites like Kickstarter. Under the rewards-based model, you offer products and services for funding and never have to repay the money. You also don't have to sell an ownership portion of your company with rewards crowdfunding. The downside is that the majority (70%) of rewards crowdfunding campaigns raise less than $10,000 while equity crowdfunding campaigns can easily raise millions.

How to Get Equity Crowdfunding for your Business

Just as with rewards-based crowdfunding, there is a process for raising small business funding through equity crowdfunding. Unlike rewards crowdfunding, where almost anyone can run a campaign on their own, you will need legal counsel to help you with the regulatory paperwork for equity crowdfunding.

The regulatory process for raising money through equity crowdfunding may include some audited financial documents, a review of your business assets and income. Raising money through the older type of equity crowdfunding to accredited investors will require that you have a system in place to verify their income or net worth. You'll also have to fill out platform-specific forms to get your campaign on one of the websites though these are usually pretty easy to complete.

Equity crowdfunding platforms have in-house staff to help you through some of the regulatory documents but you'll need to hire outside counsel for other documents and to audit your financial statements. These costs can generally run into the tens of thousands of dollars but are part of the process to raise hundreds of thousands or even millions.

Convincing investors to join your campaign is similar to what we talked about in the article on angel investors. You will need to forecast your potential for sales over the next few years, as well as expenses and profits. Equity crowdfunding investors are not generally as strict as angel investors or venture capital firms so you might not have to show projected returns of five-times within five years but you should be able to show that the company can grow by more than 20% a year for the foreseeable future.

Since your business will be raising money for itself, rather than having an investment bank push the deal out to investors, you will need to market the campaign. You will want to start by reaching out to the larger investor groups and firms on the equity crowdfunding platform. Getting support from these professional groups provides the social proof you will need to get investments from individual investors.

Equity Crowdfunding Example

I interviewed Tim Nemeckay of Mine Shaft Brewing last year after his company successfully raised $650,000 from investors on EquityNet. After this first round of development funding, the company has since gone on to raising nearly $3 million of its $9.4 million second funding round.

Mine Shaft Brewing needed funds to bypass the traditional model of craft brewing that can take years to reach production of just a few thousand barrels of beer. The equity crowdfunding campaign helped Mine Shaft start at 60,000 barrels of production capacity and rank as a top 50 craft brewer. The company was able to reach production capacity of more than 100,000 barrels within the first two years.

Tim raised money through friends and his business network before the crowdfunding campaign. He felt it was important to show that a large network of investors believed in the business before taking it to a larger crowd.

Through his equity crowdfunding campaign, Tim was able to connect with the same investor groups that helped get the Sam Adams brewing company off the ground. Most of the large equity crowdfunding sites are closely followed by large angel groups and investment firms. They use smaller crowdfunding deals to test out a company before making larger investments in the future.

EquityNet charged a quarterly fee of $507 during the campaign, which ran for three months for the initial funding. The follow-on funding ran for a little over a year and raised millions. Equity crowdfunding platforms generally either charge a monthly fee of a few hundred or a percentage of funds raised.

Tim highlighted the need for a strong team on your equity crowdfunding campaign along with investor materials. The company added up to 10 advisors from its investors and trade organizations to help consult ahead of the crowdfunding campaign. These advisors are less costly than hiring full-time executives but can really help develop your financial statements and business strategy.

Tim also suggested a 'funnel' process for finding and building relationships with investors.

- Identify investor types and demographics from early supporters to your business

- Network with investor groups and local organizations for pre-launch community building

- Build credibility through financial reports and white papers on topics around the industry

- Reach out to big-money investors from the crowdfunding sites and any local groups

- Update your network and introduce new investors, especially ones from any angel groups, to build social proof

Setting Realistic Goals for your Small Business Funding

By the time you come to equity crowdfunding as a part of the small business funding process, you should have some sales and have built a customer base. Using earlier stages like peer lending or rewards-crowdfunding to get your business to this point will make it much easier to raise money through an equity deal. It is possible to fund a startup through equity crowdfunding but investors generally like to see some proof that you can be successful.

The average deal size for equity crowdfunding ranges from $800,000 to $1.6 million depending on which platform you select. Just as with rewards crowdfunding, consider staggering your financing needs in equity crowdfunding. You might look for $1 million in your first round to expand production nationally or for working capital while waiting for a second round of financing to expand internationally. Planning multiple financing rounds will help ensure you reach smaller goals and don't have to wait on funding.

Equity crowdfunding can be used as an exit for earlier investors or as add-on financing. Besides the investment funding, crowdfunding offers the potential to add strong experience to the team through professional business groups. I have talked to more than one business that was also connected to distributors and others in the supply chain through equity crowdfunding.

A lot of business owners have chosen to use equity crowdfunding instead of seeking financing from angel investors or venture groups. Equity crowdfunding has gone a long way to democratizing small business funding and opening up the way to success for many entrepreneurs. Whatever path you choose to fund your small business, check out the complete series to better understand all your options.

Equity Crowdfunding Tips to Remember:

- As with seeking funds from angel groups, you may decide that you don't want to sell an ownership position and don't want to raise capital through equity crowdfunding. It can raise millions in funding but the same can be done through rewards crowdfunding several campaigns.

- If you decide to seek funding through equity crowdfunding, be prepared to spend tens of thousands in legal and advisor fees. You should be able to make this money back in the funding but there will be costs to preparing the documents for a campaign.

- Reach out to investor groups on the equity platform before the campaign for a pre-launch round of funding. These initial funders will add decades of experience and social proof to your company, making the campaign much more certain.

- As with rewards-based crowdfunding, consider a smaller funding goal for your first round of equity crowdfunding. Investors in this round are going to require higher rates on debt or the higher potential for returns to become involved. Use a smaller round of funding to jumpstart your business and get it ready for later stages of funding.

10 Myths and Mistakes about Starting a Business

More than 500,000 new businesses are started in America every year but just half survive longer than five years. More than half the working population works in one of the 28 million small businesses across the country. Making your business a success story is about avoiding the biggest business myths and mistakes.

Avoid these business myths and mistakes and you'll be rewarded with a strong sense of fulfillment and the potential for financial freedom. Ignore the hurdles that trip up so many owners and you'll become just another business statistic.

Business Myth #1 A Great Product Sells Itself

This is one of the most frustrating business myths and most marketers might say the opposite, "you can sell a turd with a good marketing strategy."

It can be hugely frustrating knowing you've got a great product that really meets a customer need but nobody seems to care. You sit at your storefront, virtual or traditional, daily but nobody is buying.

You must put together a good marketing strategy to get your product in front of potential customers. The big businesses do this by blasting their message everywhere through commercials but unless you've got billions for marketing, your strategy is going to be social.

Your business needs its own website and social networking profiles like Facebook, LinkedIn and Twitter. You'll share your message out across your personal profiles as well but your business needs to develop its own brand.

Start a simple website with Blue Host WordPress hosting to feature your business in detail. You can use social media management software like Hootsuite to schedule messages about your business and keep a constant stream of information going out to potential customers.

Don't forget to take advantage of offline marketing as well. Build personal relationships face-to-face and then take those contacts online into your social strategy. People you know personally are much more likely to share your message online.

Business Myth #2 Starting a Business is a Way to Escape the Rat Race

Starting a business is a good way to be eaten by the rats! This business myth is one of the most widely held and a lot of small biz owners quit their day job before understanding how much work is actually involved running your own gig.

A Gallup poll found that nearly half (49%) of the self-employed in America work more than 44 hours a week and one in four report working more than 60 hours a week.

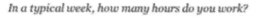

In a typical week, how many hours do you work?

■ % Less than 35 hours ■ % 35-44 hours ▓ % More than 44 hours

Aggregated results from surveys conducted each August, 2006-2009

GALLUP POLL

Launching and running your own business is hard work and there's no guarantee of success. The money might be there eventually but you'll work your butt off for it.

The upside is that your hard work can pay off and most people report a strong sense of fulfillment from running their own business. Start your company from a passion for your product or service and you'll enjoy work a lot more than punching a time card.

Business Myth #3 Entrepreneurs have to be Risk-takers

Starting a business doesn't have to put your family at risk of financial ruin. You hear often of the serial entrepreneurs and their success stories after multiple failed businesses. What you don't hear about is the amount of planning that went into each and the financial cushion they had going into their ideas.

At a conference last year, one speaker related a business idea as a leap you just had to take even in the face of uncertainty. This might be fine for someone that has already been hugely successful and built a massive following of supporters but won't work for the average person trying to support their family.

Start your business slow, maybe as freelance work until you can make it a full-time career. You'll learn a lot about marketing and running your company in the first year. Starting your business as a freelance gig also helps to understand if you really want to do it as a full-time career.

Business Myth #4 I Love my Hobby so it Will Make a Good Business

While I often talk about starting your hobby-job and that your passion will help make you successful, there is an important warning here.

Do anything as a full-time job and it will become a job. You'll still enjoy what you do but there will be times when you don't want to do it.

I love talking about investments, business and personal finance. I am a fairly quick writer and can generally put together an article in a few hours. When I was only writing 10 hours a week, I could sit back and leisurely put something together over a few days.

Managing four blogs plus writing as a freelance investment analyst now means I write upwards of 30 pages a week and must always be putting together the next idea. It's more than passion or a love of the job that gets me out of bed every morning, it's the fact that if I'm not working…I'm not getting paid.

Business Myth #5 Don't Overthink your Business, Just Do It!

If you can't get to a place where you're really comfortable with your business planning, there might be a reason for it. Some business owners will get stuck in the planning phase, letting fear of failure keep them from ever getting started. Others will rush through their business plan and quit their day job without understanding the path forward.

Avoiding this business myth is about balance and I'm afraid there is really no way to be sure if you're ready. I would say that it's much better to be over-prepared than to not know what you're getting but don't let that keep you from starting.

Business Mistake #1 Relying on Others for Answers

Too many business owners rely completely on third-party information or stuff they find on the internet. Fact check all the information that goes into your business plan and do at least a few surveys of your market. Talk directly with potential suppliers and buyers.

Doing your own research will not only help you understand how your business is going to work, it will make you an expert in the area and make you a resource to the industry.

Business Mistake #2 Only Looking for One Source of Funding

Too many business owners drain their own savings, get denied for a traditional bank loan and then go bankrupt. Planning out your sources of funding is a critical part of being successful.

Sources of fund include personal loans and unsecured business loans to get your started. Personal loans are generally easier to get and can be paid off early without a penalty. Traditional bank lending to small businesses is down 20% since 2008 with alternative finance through peer lending stepping in to fill the gap.

After the initial source of funds to get you started, use crowdfunding as a way to blend marketing with your funding needs. Crowdfunding is a great way to launch your idea and build out your product with customer feedback before you even create it.

Once you need larger sources of funding, into the millions of dollars, you'll look to angel investors and venture capitalists to take your business to the next level.

Business funding is much more a continual process than a one-and-done need. Learn how to take advantage of multiple types of funding to secure your business goals.

Each year, *Inc.* magazine lists the 5,000 fastest growing companies in America. In 2014, the Kauffman Foundation surveyed firms listed by *Inc.* since 1996 to learn about their sources of funding.

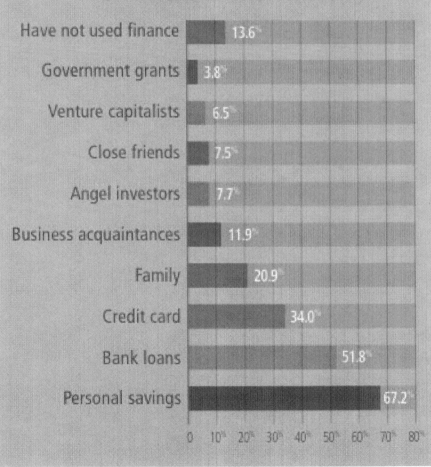

INC. FAST-GROWING FIRMS
SOURCES OF FUNDING

Source	Percentage
Have not used finance	13.6%
Government grants	3.8%
Venture capitalists	6.5%
Close friends	7.5%
Angel investors	7.7%
Business acquaintances	11.9%
Family	20.9%
Credit card	34.0%
Bank loans	51.8%
Personal savings	67.2%

0   10%   20%   30%   40%   50%   60%   70%   80%

Business Mistake #3 Not Letting your Business Evolve with Market

How can Rolling Stones keep doing it? The band was formed in 1962 but is just as popular after more than 50 years. They've got platinum albums older than most other rock stars.

It's because they let their music evolve along with the market. The Stones are belting out the same psychedelic sounds of the 60s, they listened to the market and let their sound evolve.

Let your business plan evolve as well. Your business plan isn't something you write out and then file away forever. The plan is what's called a living document because it constantly changes and grows according to your experience. Business isn't what you want, it's what your customer wants.

Business Mistake #4 Going it alone

Working alone doesn't work. Any large business will need the expertise of a team and will be more work than one person can handle.

Even a one-person shop will benefit from outsourcing some tasks to an assistant or a freelancer. Don't try to be manager, marketer, graphics design and logistics all in one. Understand your specific skill set and find others that do their own job really well.

Start building out your team of experts before you need them. They don't have to be full-time or even contracted employees but have a list of talent you can go to when you need it.

Business Mistake #5 Taking Failure Personally

A lot of business owners take it personally when their friends and community don't support their business. They end up resenting others and blame them for the business failing.

There are a lot of reasons why a business fails and it's rarely because someone wanted you to fail. What was in it for them? Did the product really fulfill a need or solve a problem and was it priced right?

Spend time researching your closest competitors and others in the same industry to understand what makes their business successful. Construct a business plan from what you know about their business and compare it to your own.

Small Business Funding Resources

This last chapter will help you get started with links to some of the best resources for funding and small business development. Not all of the small business funding resources will be right for your company but you should be able to find a few that will work for your needs.

Small Business Funding Resources for Loans

Lending Club

Lending Club is becoming the favorite for small business funding and p2p loans. The peer lending platform has helped fund more than $11 billion personal and business loans with nearly $2 billion just in the last three months. Business loans are available for up to $300,000 but you generally need to be in business for two years and have sales of $75,000 or more per year.

Even if you don't qualify for a business loan, personal loans are available for up to $35,000 with rates from 5.9% depending on your credit score.

Avant Credit

One of the biggest complaints I hear about peer lenders is the strict credit score requirements, upwards of 640 FICO on sites like Prosper and Lending Club. Avant specializes in providing personal loans for borrowers with a credit score as low as 580 FICO. Rates will be a little higher so make sure you have a plan for paying off the loan early through crowdfunding or business sales.

ACCION USA

ACCION is a private, non-profit organization that offers small business funding through loans of up to $25,000 that might not be able to get a traditional loan. The organization specializes in microloans, especially those to businesses owned by women or minorities. The site also offers small business funding workshops to help you get started.

Wells Fargo Small Business Loans

If you can get traditional bank funding then the rates are probably going to be the lowest available. Wells Fargo offers fixed-rate business loans and lines of credit. Business loans are for two to five years and from $10,000 to $100,000 with a $150 documentation fee.

Small Business Funding Resources for Factoring and Grants

CIT Factoring

There are many companies that provide factoring services though CIT is one of the largest so I've linked it here. If you sell goods on credit, then a factoring company will buy those receivables and pay you cash. You won't get the full amount of the receivables but it is a way to keep cash flowing for your business without having to wait for buyers to pay you.

Small Business Administration Loans & Grants

SBA loans are offered through traditional bank lenders but the SBA website is a good resource for information on the specific loan types. If you can structure your business to develop under non-profit research, you might try getting a grant which you won't have to repay. Otherwise, small business loans are available for general business purposes, microloans, real estate, equipment and disaster relief.

Your best bet for government grants is at the local or state-level. These might be referred to as discretionary incentive funds in your state. Connect with local business groups to get an idea of where to look for these grants and funding resources. To get you started, try the Refine Digital list of small business resources for organizations in each state.

Investor Resources for Equity Capital

AngelList

AngelList is an online platform for angel investors and has helped nearly 600 small businesses raise money. Investors cover the costs so there are no fees to start-ups. The site allows entrepreneurs to put their documents together and pitch investors on the platform either to a syndicate of angels or to individuals.

Besides raising money, entrepreneurs can also recruit talent from the site among the investors that have special insight into a particular industry. Your team is one of the most important aspects for small business funding and you absolutely must have a few profile team members with a track record of success.

Angel Capital Association

The ACA is North America's professional association for angel investors and counts 240 groups and 13,000 angel members. It is not really for start-up entrepreneurs but the resources on the site will give you a perspective into what angel investors look for in funding opportunities. The meet-ups and summits might also provide an opportunity to connect with angel investors in your area. Remember, angel investors tend to invest locally so focus your attention on regional groups.

National Venture Capital Association (NVCA)

The NVCA represents the venture capital industry in the United States. Like angel investors, these firms pool investor money to make early-stage funding in small businesses. The professional association counts 400 members and includes a directory that might help you get started searching for VC firms interested in your industry. Venture firms generally invest in specific industries and make larger funding decisions than do angel groups.

Small Business Funding Resources for Crowdfunding

Kickstarter

Kickstarter is the largest rewards-based crowdfunding platform in the world with more than 13 million visitors a month. Rewards-based crowdfunding is where you want to start after you've developed your idea through a small business loan. Selling your product through a crowdfunding campaign will allow you to develop your idea and build a loyal community. From there, you'll be able to show your crowdfunding success as social proof to large investors or for an equity-crowdfunding campaign.

Kickstarter charges a 5% fee on successfully funded projects and a payment processing fee of up to 5% on the funded amount. Crowdfunding involves a complete process of community building and marketing but can really get your small business to the next level. **Indiegogo** is another rewards-based crowdfunding platform that offers a flexible-funding model and comparable fees to Kickstarter.

Fundable

Fundable is a unique crowdfunding platform in that it allows both rewards-based and equity-based campaigns. I still like the larger platforms like Kickstarter or Indiegogo for rewards campaigns but Fundable might offer some advantages as a one-stop website. The site charges a flat fee of $179 per much plus the standard processing fees, possibly making it more attractive to large campaigns versus the platforms that charge a percentage of funds raised.

SeedInvest

SeedInvest is an equity-crowdfunding platform open to accredited investors. Investors pay no fees but start-ups are charged 5% of funding plus up to $5,000 for due diligence, escrow, marketing and legal expenses. The benefit to the site is that it may be better for very early stage companies since that seems to be the model.

CircleUp

CircleUp is a good equity crowdfunding platform but companies typically need to have booked sales of more than $500,000 annually or meet other requirements. The average funding time is between two and three months and can be through debt or equity securities. CircleUp has a relatively strong network of 'circles' on the platform, groups of investors that follow each other's investments. Many of these groups are started by analysts or institutional groups and can provide a boost of credibility to your company if they invest.

EquityNet

EquityNet is one of the larger and more established equity-crowdfunding platforms and has helped raise more than $300 million for start-ups through debt, equity or royalty-based offers. Entrepreneurs can raise from $10,000 to $10 million for small business funding.

National Business Incubators Association (NBIA)

Also not technically a small business funding source but a good place to start for connections to funding sources, technical support, managerial training and shared office space. Incubators, or accelerators, are professional groups that help nurture small businesses and entrepreneurs. The group can help you through consulting, professional development and networking.

More Business Resources Books

Ever wonder why 60% of crowdfunding campaigns fail while some people are able to come back to the funding source time and again to raise millions? Get the detailed process you need to be successful in a rewards-based crowdfunding campaign. Don't sell ownership of your business, get the money you need by selling products and services. Get Step-by-Step Crowdfunding and get funded!

See through the BS and scams in passive income strategies to start building a real source of income today in blogging, real estate, stocks and bonds.

NO fluff, NO theories, and NO sugar coating – just the detailed process on how I put together an income from four sources and make money whether I work or not. Click here to buy The Passive Income Myth

A Special Request

I hope you've enjoyed From Zero to Business and found the advice to be helpful in putting together your business funding strategy. Throughout the book, I've tried to put together a simple framework for developing your business idea and giving you several options for the funding you need to be successful.

I'd like to ask one favor as you finish reading the book. Reader reviews are extremely important to the success of a book on Amazon. Reviews play a big part in determining the rank of a book and how many people see it when searching.

If you found the book to be helpful, would you please leave a review on the Amazon page?

It's really easy to do and does not have to be a long, detailed review.

Please click here to leave a review on Amazon

- Just go to the book's page on Amazon (or through the link above) and click on "customer reviews" or scroll down and click on "Write a customer review"

- Your review can be as short as a sentence or as long as you like. Just try describing what you liked about the book and any particular points from a chapter.

I always appreciate honest reviews.Thank you so much!